ANOINTED FOR A PURPOSE

Confirmed for Life in the Twenty-first Century

ANOINTED FOR A PURPOSE

Confirmed for Life in the Twenty-first Century

Mary Sharon Moore

AWAKENING VOCATIONS

Eugene, Oregon

ANOINTED FOR A PURPOSE

Confirmed for Life in the Twenty-first Century

Awakening Vocations | 4150 Oak Street | Eugene OR 97405

www.awakeningvocations.com

ISBN: 13: 978-1479108916

           10: 147910891X

Front cover photo: Mary Sharon Moore.

Back cover photo: File photo, Awakening Vocations.

Manufactured in the United States of America on 30% postconsumer waste recycled material; Forest Stewardship Council (FSC)-certified.

CONTENTS

Introduction   1

Part I   BECOMING ANOINTED   7

1   Confirmation: The Name Says It All   9

2   Lifelong Relationship: God Calls, You Respond   18

3   Anointed for a Purpose: You are the Presence of the Living Christ   33

4   None of Us Stands Alone: What the Christian Community Owes You   60

Part II   LIVING THE ANOINTED LIFE   77

5   Single, Married, Celibate: A Deeper Discernment of Vocational Lifestyle   79

6   Career or Calling: Discerning the Difference   96

7   Anointed for Peacemaking: Why Peace Defines the Core of Christian Life   111

Epilogue: Why the Resistance to Confirmation? You Deserve to be Heard   127

Bibliography   133

Scripture Citations and References   137

Index   139

INTRODUCTION

Why do you and I, baptized and confirmed as we are in the Holy Spirit, do what we do? Why do we pray and strive to pray well? Why do we engage in relationships and strive to bring dignity and worth to a life shaped by such relationships? Why do we work and strive to find meaning in what we do? Why do we strive to discern God's calling—not only when we find ourselves at the threshold of adulthood but throughout the course of our lifetime?

We may stumble with our reasons and wrestle with the words that might best express this striving. Perhaps we long to succeed, or at least to somehow "get it right." Perhaps we intuitively seek our place upon the larger stage of human affairs, or at least hope to find our niche, where we can touch others' lives in some positive, caring, creative, encouraging, or liberating way.

In truth, we do seek to discern God's calling, and to come to grips with the nature of God's calling, not because we understand what we seek but because we are impelled by the Holy Spirit. We have been everlastingly sealed in this same Spirit to discern and express the ways in which Jesus, the risen Lord, continues his creative, encouraging, healing, redeeming work in our twenty-first century world. He is not yet finished with this work, and therefore neither are we.

So why *do* you and I, baptized and confirmed as we are in the Holy Spirit, do what we do? These questions of purpose are worthy questions. People who are sacramentally confirmed in the Holy Spirit are not the only ones who seek a life of meaning. Such seeking for purpose and fulfillment is deeply embedded in the human spirit—made, as we all are, in the image of God, and each of us with work to do.[1] But we who are sacramentally anointed are especially commissioned to seek and fulfill our unique work of love, compassion, and justice within the reign of God.

Therefore, these questions of purpose are *vocational* questions. We have been anointed for a purpose—a purpose that is seldom immediately clear to us, but which shapes the trajectory of our life-in-God and the trajectory of this world in which God is fully invested.

Grace upon grace, St. Paul would say of our lives, we progress "from glory to glory, as from the Lord who is the Spirit" (2 Corinthians 3:18). This progression is the lifelong unfolding of God's calling and the seldom logical, predictable, or direct path of our response. Our anointed life in the Holy Spirit, shaped by this ongoing dynamic of God's calling and our response, is the holy and living dialogue which we call "vocation."

As you will discover within these pages, *Anointed for a Purpose* will help you to more fully be yourself-in-God—that wholehearted and holy self whom God has been desiring and calling into being all along. And as the title makes clear, the holy dialogue between God and self takes on a yet deeper meaning with the anointing and consecration of your life in the church's initiating sacraments of Baptism and Confirmation. While we refer to these as "sacraments of initiation," they also are in essence the first of the vocational sacraments, drawing us into that lifelong dynamic of God's calling and our response. The initiatory and the vocational are as linked as the in-breath and the

---

[1] See Genesis 1:26–30. Unless otherwise noted, all Scripture references are to the *New American Bible* (hereafter *NAB*) (Grand Rapids, MI: Catholic World Press, 1987).

out-breath, first experienced at birth and unstoppable until the moment of our return to God.

Indeed, *Anointed for a Purpose* speaks to men and women who have experienced "a new birth to a living hope through the resurrection of Jesus Christ" (1 Peter 1:3). Equally, this resource offers encouragement and practical vocational guidance to recently confirmed youth and young adults. In fact, this is the book that I wish had been written when I was early on in my own sacramentally anointed spiritual journey.

It seems to me that for those who are baptized and anointed in the living Christ, there is, over time, either engagement in this sacramental anointing, or flight from such engagement—whether that flight be passive or intentional. We are baptized and anointed into the One who gave himself completely with selfless devotion to the most noble mission the human mind and spirit can ever imagine: restoration of humankind and of all creation to its original loveliness, beauty, creativity, and fruitfulness in the company of God. But this work of divine restoration is still underway. We are either increasingly engaged in this redemptive, restorative enterprise, or we are fleeing, even if inch by inch, from its rightful claim upon our lives. Every day offers a new decision point. And our decision for engagement defines the very core of vocation: God's calling and our authentic response.

In these pages I will be honest with you about *your* life, *your* destiny, and why the anointing you have received in Confirmation matters beyond what you may have imagined. No matter your age, claiming your place in the Christian community as surely as you claim your place in the world is a work of great spiritual importance; your place within the Christian community is the unique place from which you touch your world with the power of the Holy Spirit according to the particular ways you have been gifted.

I know with absolute certainty that as long as the church continues to anoint people in Baptism and Confirmation, and feed us in Eucharist, our church will experience no shortage of vocations. God's calling is unstoppable! The depth of Jesus' work of redemption, a work in which we participate, is unfathomable. The movement of the Holy Spirit—in our lives, in our church, and in our world—is irrepressible.

In Baptism, Confirmation, and Eucharist the Christian community is washed, anointed, fed, and spiritually equipped for work in our twenty-first century world. And this Christian community includes every member, at every stage and state in life. No one is insignificant. Indeed, every one of us is significant—in fact, a signifier, or a sacramental expression, of the dynamic presence of the risen Christ at work in the world.

These powerful sacraments of initiation were never meant to enable you to merely *imitate* Jesus. They empower you, with the full strength of his holy Spirit, to actually *stand in his place* and, with his divine authority, to reveal more fully the reign of God.[2] You can think of the sacraments of initiation as the launch pad from which God sends forth—through you to the world—mighty bursts of love, compassion, healing, justice, mercy, and peace. In short, you participate directly in the work of redemption. You are the anointed carrier of God's unstoppable love. Just as God counted on the young Virgin's wholehearted Yes, God is counting—more than you know—on *your* wholehearted Yes to your calling to a worthy work of everlasting value within the reign of God, no matter where you are in your life right now.

What you do with your life *is* important; who you are becoming matters immensely to God and to the world you touch. And the world you touch may be your immediate family, or a handful of clients; it may be co-workers, or customers you will encounter only once; the world you touch may be the audiences you have not yet met, or constituents who count on you to stand up

---

[2] Regarding the term *reign of God,* I note in the introduction to my book *Touching the Reign of God* that the term *kingdom of God* suggests the "secure consolation of place. But the *reign* of God is more verb than noun, ... the invitation and the challenge of participating in a radically new way of being." See Mary Sharon Moore, *Touching the Reign of God: Bringing Theological Reflection to Daily Life* (Eugene, OR: Wipf and Stock, 2009), xii.

and give voice to the needs of the voiceless.

Anointed for a Purpose gives you entry into a necessary conversation on the particular contours of God's unique calling of you and the quality of your personal response. Sparked by what you read here, this conversation might be interior, between you and God; it might be courageous conversation with a spouse or trusted family member, or with peers; or it might be ongoing conversation with a spiritual mentor. It is the honest, engaging, and necessary vocational conversation that will shape, animate, and sustain you through life, because your real, though hidden, conversation partner is the Holy Spirit. In Confirmation you have been anointed for a purpose: to reveal in your unique and gifted way, in your time and place in this world, nothing less than the reign of God.

PART I

BECOMING ANOINTED

What does it mean to be sacramentally anointed, smeared with the sacred chrism? Was your chrismation, your anointing into Christ, merely a rite of passage? Or has it become a lifelong invitation to enter into a new quality of relationship with the risen Lord, with his church, and therefore with your world?

Part I, Becoming Anointed, explores the nature of God's calling in your life. In these first four chapters we will view the sacrament of Confirmation through an integrative lens, and through that lens bring into clearer focus your relationship with the living Christ and your rightful and necessary place within the Christian community.

1

CONFIRMATION

The Name Says It All

Therefore, ... be all the more eager to make your call and election firm, for, in doing so, you will never stumble.

2 Peter 1:10

The New Testament scriptures have a way of hurling us into the depths of spiritual matters, hurling us directly indeed into the mystery of God. An intriguing definition of the mystery of sacramental life can be found in these words of St. Paul: "For God who said, 'Let light shine out of darkness,' has shone in our hearts to bring to light the knowledge of the glory of God on the face of [Jesus] Christ" (2 Corinthians 4:6). Just as these words point us to the *sacramental* dimension of Christian faith, St. Paul's next sentence points us equally to the *vocational* dimension of our faith: "But we hold this treasure in earthen vessels, that the surpassing power may be of God and not from us" (v. 7).

A Sacramental Context

The church teaches that sacraments (termed "mysteries" in the Eastern churches) are "efficacious signs of grace, instituted by Christ and entrusted to the church, by which divine life is dispensed to us."[3] Apart from the repeatable sacraments of Eucharist, Reconciliation, and the Anointing of the Sick, we can easily think of the other sacraments—Baptism, Confirmation, Matrimony, and Holy Orders—as one-time events. We may spend weeks or months preparing for the day we celebrate the sacrament. Here we may go through rehearsal, or at least last-minute coaching. The family gathers, often arriving from great distances, and the people receiving the sacrament are dressed up in clothes they normally would not wear. For infant baptism it's the christening gown, or for adult baptism, some white garment representing the christening gown.[4] For youth or adults being confirmed, it's the suit and tie or special dress, with uncomfortable shoes to match. With the sacrament of Matrimony the couple is decked out in bridal gown and tux; with the sacrament of Holy Orders the newly ordained are vested in priestly garments. So we think of sacraments as "special events." Indeed, they are.

But what we sometimes forget is that the power and purpose of each sacrament also *unfolds over time*.[5] God uses your entire lifetime as the context for the ever-maturing sacramental relationship into which you have entered with the risen Lord. Your ever deepening being-in-God brings that

---

[3] *Catechism of the Catholic Church*, Second edition, English translation (Washington, DC: United States Catholic Conference, 1997) (hereafter *CCC*), sec. 1131.

[4] At the Mass of Christian Burial this christening garment appears again, now in the form of the white pall draped over the coffin.

[5] I recall the chancellor of my archdiocese mentioning anecdotally how priests whom she had known as hopeful young seminarians often would come back to her a year or two after their ordination, after undergoing some profound or maturing experience in their priestly ministry, and tell her, *"Now* I understand: I am a priest." Married couples, too, have reported growing into the sacramental reality of their married life with the birth of their first child, or, sadly, with the loss of a child or some other trauma.

relationship to full flowering and to fruitbearing, so that in the course of time God can reap a bountiful harvest of love, compassion, healing, justice, mercy, and peace—yes, in short, the gleaming, fragrant harvest of redemption—in this world.

Where Confirmation Fits In

The sacrament of Confirmation is situated among the sacraments of initiation—Baptism, Confirmation, Eucharist—those sacraments that *orient your life and sustain you in your movement toward God's perfect desiring.* These initiatory sacraments are not only for your spiritual good and salvation but for the good and salvation of those whose lives you will touch in the course of your lifetime. And over your lifetime you already have touched and will touch many lives—your friends, your neighbors, perhaps a spouse and children, your children's friends and their parents, extended family, your co-workers, business associates, people in your community, fellow volunteers, those who serve you and those whom you serve in day-to-day transactions, and even complete strangers whom you encounter but whose names you may never know.

So the sacrament of Confirmation serves as a foundation for a *continuum of spiritual growth* as your life unfolds and matures. This hidden yet sure process of God's life at work within you, divine light pouring out of darkness, begins with Baptism. It is God's life already at work within you that is confirmed or *affirmed and made strong* in this sacrament we call Confirmation. This sacramental anointing gives you the spiritual and moral strength to confirm or profess, with ever greater conviction throughout the course of your life, that you live for God's purposes.[6]

You can look at this continuum of God's life at work in you in this

---

[6] See Romans 14:8: "For if we live, we live for the Lord, and if we die, we die for the Lord." This understanding that we belong entirely to God, for God's purposes, is what we affirm and profess by virtue of the power of our anointing in Baptism and more robustly proclaim in Confirmation.

way: You are *from* God; you are *for* God; you are *returning to* God.[7] What does this continuum mean?

Trajectory of the Anointed Life

First, you are *from* God. Your spiritual journey started long before you were born, with God's eternal desiring of you—yes, *you*—to stand in Jesus' place and touch the world with his touch, in *this* place and time.[8] The risen Lord spoke a startling and sobering word to those first apostles: "As the Father has sent me, so I send you" (John 20:21). In a very real sense we can say that Jesus truly is the first and preeminent Apostle, blazing the way for those who would follow him, the well-beloved Son sent to carry out his Father's willing.[9] Jesus was very clear that he did not come in his own name but in his Father's name.[10] From the beginning of his public ministry[11] to his final breath at his execution,[12] Jesus understood that he was from God, sent to fulfill his earthly mission of unleashing his Father's unimaginably generous plan—the reclaiming of humankind for everlasting communion at the table of the triune God. As Jesus is *from* God, so you are *from* God.

---

[7] This understanding of the dynamic of God's calling runs through the coauthored works of Francis Kelly Nemeck, OMI, and Marie Theresa Coombs. See their *Called by God: A Theology of Vocation and Lifelong Commitment* (Eugene, OR: Wipf and Stock, 2001) and *Discerning Vocations to Marriage, Celibacy and Singlehood* (Eugene, OR: Wipf and Stock, 2001) (hereafter *Discerning Vocations*).

[8] A friend of mine who is a steadfast advocate for victims of human trafficking expressed her unease that her life seems so whole and peaceful and not caught in the vortex of enslavement, degradation, and ever-present oppression. "Did God make a mistake?" I asked. "No," she had to admit. I reminded her, "You use your freedom and privilege to stand up and press for the cause of these voiceless ones. *You stand in the place of Jesus.*" She replied, "I had never thought of it in that way." She thinks of it in that way now.

[9] See, for example, John 8:26 ("[T]he one who sent me is true, and what I heard from him I tell the world"); John 18:37 ("For this I was born and for this I came into the world, to testify to the truth"); and in these clear and direct words, John 4:34 ("My food is to do the will of the one who sent me").

[10] See John 5:43: "I came in the name of my Father." Jesus' clarity on who sent him throws his adversaries into unclarity on the source of what they claim as their authority.

[11] See Luke 3:21–22, the baptism of Jesus; see also Luke 4:16–21, where Jesus reads—and missionally identifies with—the passage from Isaiah (see Isaiah 61:1–2) regarding the messiah's restoration of Zion.

[12] See Luke 23:46: "Father, into your hands I commend my spirit."

If you were born into a Christian family and baptized at an early age, you perhaps have entertained the thought, at least once in your lifetime, that Baptism was the church's way of committing you to something before you could even see whether you wanted to "buy in" to it or not. Smart shoppers that we are, we not only look for the best value, we search for the cheapest deals. But a consumer's approach to Baptism and a life of Christian faith short-changes God's grace and completely misses the gift of this extraordinary relationship. Rather, Baptism sets in motion *God's* perfect desiring and perfect plan for your life. The deep sacramental work of Baptism creates capacity in you for the only freedom that can really set you free: the freedom to be your real, authentic self-in-God. All people are *from* God; through Baptism you are enabled to make a lifelong and fruitful profession of this amazing and unexplainable grace.

Second, you are *for* God. Jesus was very clear that his life was lived at the service of his Father's willing. Referring to himself as both shepherd and sheep gate, Jesus says, "I came so that [you] might have life and have it more abundantly."[13] Your spiritual continuum progresses as God's desiring becomes expressed in the unique person whom you are, with all your gifting and limitations, all your dreams and resistances. God's willing becomes expressed in actual, perceivable ways as you apply *all* your heart, soul, mind, and strength[14] to the circumstances of your life. Amazingly, God's desiring for your life finds its way through all the noise, confusion, distractions, skewed decision making, and morally complex choices that shape your life. Jesus' words cut straight to the heart of the matter: "It was not you who chose me, but I who chose you and appointed you to go and bear fruit that will remain" (John 15:16). And, amazingly,

---

[13] See John 10:10. See also John 10:15: "I will lay down my life for the sheep." The shepherd typically would not be the owner of the herd but, as in the case of young David, a son entrusted with stewarding this portion of the family's wealth. A mere "hired hand" could not be trusted to defend the herd in times of danger (see John 10:12).

[14] See Mark 12:30 for Jesus' teaching on the Greatest Commandment; see parallels at Matthew 22:37, and Luke 10:27 (where the scholar questioning Jesus on the greatest commandment gives the reply). The phrase originally appears in Deuteronomy 6:5.

Jesus seems pleased to choose you *where you are in your life right now* to join him in his mission of redemption and joy. He never said you have to "pretty up" your life before he is willing to work with you. As we recall, the risen Lord had a way of walking through locked doors to break through to his apostles who were clutched with fear.[15]

Your *being for* God—your standing firm in God—is a lived expression of the sacrament of Confirmation. More fully, you are *working for* God, not as someone works for a demanding boss, but as a full-share participant in Jesus' work of redeeming and restoring the world to right and loving relationship with his Father. You are anointed for privileged work. In fact, this privileged work is called "priestly work," the work of being the intercessor, the go-between, as Moses was, as Jesus was most perfectly, the holy bridge between God's perfect willing and the world as you encounter it today.

You accomplish this bridge work, this priestly work, not on your own but by the guidance of the Holy Spirit, and in a living relationship with the Christian community. People who are not baptized certainly can do good works—and they do, every day, because unbaptized people also are from God, and their lives hold great capacity to express God's love and care and provision. But you have the Holy Spirit, enabling you to give your intentional and wholehearted Yes to *being for* God, and actively and intentionally working to reveal God's inexhaustible love and right order here and now. You rightly can expect results that reveal God's hand and God's heart.

Finally, you are *returning to* God. The continuum of God's eternal desiring for your life reaches its fulfillment when you pass from life through death to the eternal banquet of the Holy Trinity. We get a glimpse of this continuum still in progress following Jesus' resurrection but before he has

---

[15] See John 20:19, 26.

returned to his Father.[16] There *will* come a day—at the time when your life on earth is completed—when the Christian community will present your life to God, the good seed that has died so that God can now reap the harvest.[17] What does this final returning to God mean for you right now, in light of your being baptized and confirmed in Christ Jesus?

Quite simply, it means that you are washed and anointed for partnership with God in the most privileged work you can imagine—standing in the place of the risen Lord here and now, guided and fortified by his holy Spirit, to make of *your world* a pleasing offering to God. This is the priestly assignment of all who are sacramentally anointed. Your initiation into Christ Jesus and into the community of the church is not a one-time event but the continually renewing source of God's calling of you—your vocation. Your participation in Eucharist brings you again and again to that vocational source, the headwaters, if you will, of the mighty river of God's willing and of God's life coursing through the ages. Faithfully presenting yourself, ready for work, fully disposed to God's willing, *is* your vocation right now, your faithful response to God's calling. By the grace and anointing which you have received in Confirmation, your whole life is both preparing for and an expression of your spiritual fruitfulness and your eventual returning to God.

Confirmation in a Nutshell

What can we say at this point about the sacrament of Confirmation? We know three things for certain:

---

[16] See John 20:17, where the risen Lord says to the beloved Mary of Magdala, "Stop holding on to me, for I have not yet ascended to the Father." In essence, he warns: Do not cling to what you think you know of me; or, more simply and more broadly, *Do not cling to what you think you know.*

[17] See John 12:24. I work with this image of "God reaping the harvest" in my essay, "Your Attitude Must be Christ's," in *Touching the Reign of God,* 19.

1. Confirmation means being *personally called forth and anointed in God's intention for your life.* This calling forth occurs for you personally, but always within the Christian community, and this sacramental anointing which is for your sanctification is also for the sake of others, for the sake of this world which God still so loves. God's calling is expressed in your life according to the particular ways that God has gifted you.

2. Confirmation sets in motion *your standing firm with God,* anointed as you are in the power of the Holy Spirit to actually stand in the place of Jesus in order to unleash his immeasurable good for the part of the world which you uniquely touch.

3. Confirmation, ultimately, is *God's* Yes to you, to your life, your purpose, and your destiny. The sacrament of Confirmation is also *your* Yes to your life, purpose, and destiny, even though you have no way of really knowing what this means. Your *not* knowing with absolute certainty your exact purpose and destiny is not an obstacle for God, so do not let it be an obstacle for you.

We have explored what Confirmation means in the context of the sacraments of initiation and the Christian community. Next we will look at Confirmation in the context of your lifelong relationship with God and your relationship with this world which God still so loves.

Questions for Conversation

1.   What two or three points can I glean from this chapter?

2.   Given the circumstances of my life, what does this phrase mean for me: to be *empowered to stand in the place of Christ Jesus in my world?* In what situations—no matter how small or insignificant—have I actually felt that I was standing in the place of the risen Lord? (Be specific with the details, and look for recurring patterns.)

3.   How am I currently standing in Jesus' place for the good of others? Who are they? What am I actually doing when I stand in his place? What is this experience like for me?

4.   How do I picture myself standing in the place of Jesus in the future? Will I be pursuing certain studies? or growing professionally in ways that will position me to stand more responsibly or effectively in his place? Am I a parent to young children who one day will be teens? or a parent to teens who soon will be young adults? (Describe as fully as possible.)

2

LIFELONG RELATIONSHIP

God Calls, You Respond

Always be ready to give an explanation to anyone who asks you
for a reason for your hope.

1 Peter 3:15

While Confirmation may seem like a one-time event, the truth is, as a
sacrament, Confirmation is powerful enough to become for you *an anointed way
of living.* In fact, the anointing you receive in Confirmation is the powerful
means by which you will become fully your self-in-God. This sacramental
anointing launches you into your lifelong work of *christification,* which St. Paul
describes as God's deep work of bringing you to your full stature in Christ.[18]

---

[18] See Ephesians 4:13: "… until we all attain to the unity of faith and knowledge of the Son of God,
to mature [personhood], to the extent of the full stature of Christ." Importantly, St. Paul makes the
point that this work of christification, or achieving this "full stature of Christ," does not happen for
the believer independently but within the gifted body of believers united as "one body and one
Spirit, as you were also called to the one hope of your call" (v. 4).

2 | LIFELONG RELATIONSHIP

The scandal of God's generosity is that by virtue of God's anointing of you, and your steadfast response, you are destined to eventually *become Christ,* as St. Paul points out repeatedly. You already are in the process of achieving this fullness of God's calling, your life rendered both fruitful and hidden in Christ. We recall in the words handed down to us from St. Augustine, *Become what you eat: The body of Christ.* These words speak an unimaginable yet inescapable truth of divine indwelling within you to the point, eventually, of your complete identification with the living Christ—your christification.

The Goal of Confirmation: Life in Christ

Père Teilhard de Chardin, the twentieth century French Jesuit, referred to this work of christification, where Christ becomes all in all,[19] when he wrote, in *Hymn of the Universe*: "Lord, lock me up in the deepest depths of your heart; and then, holding me there, burn me, purify me, … till I become utterly what you would have me be …."[20] These spiritually are very strong and challenging words, no doubt about it. And concerning the christification of all the world, Teilhard added this prayer: "What I discern in [you] is simply a furnace of fire; and the more I fix my gaze on [it] … the only features I can distinguish in you are those of the face of a world which has burst into flame."[21] These words speak of a reality to which we have barely awakened. Quoting the prophet Isaiah, St. Paul humbly observes: "What eye has not seen, and ear has not heard, / and what has not entered the human heart, / what God has prepared for those who love him" (1 Corinthians 2:9). In the end, the living Christ will *be* all, *in* all.

Twentieth century Trappist monk and writer Thomas Merton alluded to this christification-in-progress when describing the notion of what he termed *le*

---

[19] See 1 Corinthians 15:28: "When everything is subjected to him, then the Son himself will [also] be subjected to the One who subjected everything to him, so that God will be all in all."

[20] Pierre Teilhard de Chardin, SJ, *Hymn of the Universe* (New York: Harper & Row, 1961), 32.

[21] Ibid., 34.

point vierge within the human soul, that "point of pure truth, a point or spark which belongs entirely to God, … the pure glory of God in us. … It is like a pure diamond, blazing with the invisible light of heaven."[22] This all is the work of christification, begun in each of us at some unnamable point in eternity and brought to fruition by the Holy Spirit.

This sacrament of Confirmation is so powerful that if you were to give your complete and unqualified Yes to this anointing of the Holy Spirit, your life would open up in ways you could not have imagined. The young virgin Mary, in giving her complete and unqualified Yes, foreshadowed what our lives too are meant to look like and what they too are meant to bear. There is no magic in this anointing, nor is there anything automatic, just because you have gone through the rite of Confirmation. Each of us must *work with* the Holy Spirit—who is the hidden power within this sacrament—in a conscious, intentional way, not just on the day of Confirmation but every day as we mature through life.[23]

Source of All Relationships

This steadfast relationship of indwelling of the Holy Spirit shapes and animates all of our other relationships. This indwelling of the Holy Spirit is, in fact, the interior and hidden source from which all worthwhile relationships

---

[22] Thomas Merton, *Conjectures of a Guilty Bystander,* in *Thomas Merton: Spiritual Master: The Essential Writings,* ed., with introduction, Lawrence S. Cunningham (New York: Paulist, 1992), 146.

[23] I distinctly recall, at age forty-five, sitting in bed one Saturday morning, enjoying unrushed time for coffee, reading, journaling, and prayer. And with unexplainable lightning bolt clarity I suddenly understood that I had never actually asked the Holy Spirit to be the active agent in my life. I was stunned, chagrined, and found myself hurled spiritually and immediately into action to remedy this gap. What I also understood was that this lightning bolt of awareness was not my doing but was itself a sure stirring of the Holy Spirit, who could wait no longer for my waking up. As Sr. Helen Prejean, writer and advocate for alternatives to the death penalty in the United States, wisely notes, "If we are awake—and it's all about waking—we are called to play a significant role in the healing of the world. … When we wake up it is always a grace. Waking up is always a gift. It doesn't matter when you wake up. You just start living from there." From a talk titled "The Promise of Restorative Justice" (sponsored by the Appropriate Dispute Resolution Center, the Clark Honors College, and the Savage Endowment for International Relations and Peace, University of Oregon School of Law, Eugene, OR, October 19, 2010).

flow.[24] This indwelling, or abiding or remaining in the Holy Spirit, is the actual lived experience which Jesus urged upon his followers: "Remain in me, as I remain in you. ... As the Father loves me, so I also love you. Remain in my love" (John 15:4a, 9).[25] This is Jesus' irresistible invitation to vocational fulfillment: everlasting communion in God. On the night before his arrest and execution Jesus revealed the deep vocational nature of this divine indwelling within the human experience: "I ... pray ... for the ones you [Father] have given me, because they are yours. ... Holy Father, keep them in your name that you have given me, so that they may be one just as we are" (John 17:9–11).

Jesus expanded his prayer for this relationship of intimate indwelling, that it might ripple and swell outward throughout the ages: "I pray not only for them, but also for those who will believe in me ... that they may all be one, as you, Father, are in me and I in you, that they also may be in us, ... that they may be brought to perfection as one. ... I wish that where I am they also may be with me" (John 17:20–24). Jesus fully understood that because of the Holy Spirit's indwelling, in a redeemed world there is, for his followers, no separation from God.[26] This vocational understanding, and the strength and consolation which it gave Jesus within the divine-human relationship, especially before his death, shaped every dimension of his life and mission. Jesus yearns for each of us to have this vocational understanding, too, so that our relationship with God will become a source of strength, especially in our own times of severe testing, and more effectively define and shape every dimension of our lives.

The risen Lord made this divine-human indwelling available to each of us when he walked through the locked doors of that upper room and breathed

---

[24] This understanding of the Holy Spirit as the source of all worthwhile relationships becomes especially important in discerning vocational lifestyle, discussed in chapter 5.

[25] In chapter 15 of St. John's Gospel, Jesus uses this term "remain" twelve times. A search of Jesus' use of the word "remain" and similar terms ("abide" and "dwell") in this indwelling sense reveals 19 occurrences in St. John's Gospel. See James Strong, STD, LLD, *The New Strong's Exhaustive Concordance of the Bible* (hereafter *Concordance*) (Nashville: Thomas Nelson Publishers, 1996), s.vv. "Remain," "Abide," "Dwell."

[26] This is the point which Zooey makes to his spiritually distraught college-age sister Franny, in J. D. Salinger's book *Franny and Zooey* (New York: Bantam, 1961, 1969), 170.

forth the gift of his holy Spirit on those early followers. This breath of God, the Holy Spirit, has been faithfully passed on through the generations, the holy flame of God's love kept alive and burning brightly in the lives of God's faithful people, right up to the present day.[27]

Jesus has Opened the Door

In this divine-human relationship of lifelong indwelling, God will continually beckon, and one way or another you will continually respond. The power and spiritual fragrance of the sacrament of Confirmation unfolds over the course of your life as you mature and become more responsible for your relationship with Jesus and more committed to his mission, within the context of the Christian community. In the Gospels we find Jesus' closest followers taking ever greater risk in their relationship with him, and assuming ever greater responsibility in shouldering their part in his mission.[28] You can expect to experience this same relational dynamic. In fact, "receiving confirmation" of God's calling for your life sets in motion the most important and life-shaping relationship you will ever know. God will always be the initiator, and your work will always be to faithfully and obediently respond.[29] Apart from God, none of us can come up with anything new—no brilliant ideas, no great initiatives. We are so dependent on God that not even our desire to do good is our own. It is

---

[27] I heard it said that as the early church grew and spread out geographically, the bishop was no longer able to personally anoint and initiate people into the faith, so he would breathe the breath of the Holy Spirit into a box, close the lid, and a courier—possibly a deacon—would run with the box to the waiting community where he would open the box and release the breath of the Holy Spirit.

[28] See Matthew 10:1; Mark 6:7; and Luke 9:1–2, where Jesus gives the Twelve authority and sends them out; and Luke 10:1–12, where Jesus appoints "seventy others," and gives them authority to heal and proclaim the reign of God. See also John 6:60–68, where many of Jesus' followers decide that they cannot accept the radical, veil-ripping truth of divine intimacy to which he invites them. Jesus asks the Twelve, "Do you also want to leave?" And Peter, recognizing that they are far too given to identification with their Lord to turn away, replies, "Master, to whom shall we go? You have the words of eternal life" (v. 68).

[29] I use the terms "faithfulness" and "obedience" often in the vocational context, invoking the deeper aspect of this term *obedience:* to "listen with the ear of the heart," or simply, "with a listening heart." See 1 Kings 3:9, where King Solomon prays for "an understanding heart," or a heart that listens to God's willing in order to serve God's people.

God's desire within us. *Everything* is from God.[30] The Holy Spirit plants every worthy idea and sets in motion every worthy initiative, giving you stewardship as though each idea or initiative were your own. And it is the Holy Spirit who nudges every good work forward, bringing it to fruition in due time, according to God's perfect plan.

Where Prayer Fits In

If God is always the initiator, then does prayer even matter? This is a worthy question, a frequent and honest question, and it deserves an honest answer. If God knows the master plan, where *does* your prayer meaningfully fit into this lifelong relationship of divine call and human response? The question, "Does my prayer matter?" leads us down to the root of authentic prayer—prayer that comes from God and is fulfilled in God, yet requires our active participation.

The most powerful passage I know in Scripture about prayer is found in St. Paul's letter to the Romans. He reminds us that through the movement of the Holy Spirit in the human heart, God again is the initiator: "the Spirit … comes to the aid of our weakness; for we do not know how to pray as we ought, but the Spirit itself intercedes with inexpressible groanings" (Romans 8:26). This passage does not imply that we all should be praying in tongues or that we even *need* to be praying in tongues. But St. Paul does urge us to get out of the way to let the Holy Spirit pray real prayer in us. We need to let go of our prayer agenda in order to make space in our lives for God's greater plan, praying earnestly not that "*my* will" but that "*thy* will" be done.[31]

---

[30] For more on this notion of humankind's absolute poverty-of-being and complete dependence on God, see Johannes Metz's inspiring and classic meditation, *Poverty of Spirit* (Mahwah, NJ: Paulist Press, 1968, 1998).

[31] I do not mean to imply that all prayer becomes "spontaneous," or leaves us wondering, "Where did *that* come from?" Having prayed the Liturgy of the Hours steadfastly for nearly forty years, I continue to feel as though I am plunging fresh into the mystery of God with each praying of the

When you surrender deeply to God in prayer, you do not need to know what you are saying or what your words mean. You do not need to remember the content of your prayer once you rise and go about your day. You do not need to know where your prayer will lead you, or what action it will prompt you to take. It is God's work to reveal that, when God deems the time and the circumstances are right. Your work is to let the Holy Spirit form the words, or the "groanings," as St. Paul says, and allow the Holy Spirit to pray through you. In essence, you possess the power to set the Holy Spirit free to pray through you, a formidable power indeed, and one not to be taken lightly but to be put to full use. (Conversely, you also hold the power to resist the Holy Spirit, but it takes far more effort, with no reward, to push back against the intention of the Spirit and against the joy of God's desiring in you.)

How does the Holy Spirit pray through you? How does it work? For example, in your intercessory prayer you might find yourself praying, simply enough, "for the needs of the world." And then recent images of war-torn areas might come to mind, or you might recall accounts of families, or entire neighborhoods, or entire regions devastated by tornado, earthquake, or deadly sea waves. Or as you pray "for the needs of the world" you might unexpectedly find yourself thinking of something you recently read about those who dedicate their lives to speaking out for justice, or recalling a news story you heard of medical teams who quickly responded to people injured by natural disaster or wounded in war. Or as you pray "for the needs of the world" you might envision young people mobilizing their youthful energy and imagination and spirit to stand firm against violence or oppression.

In the midst of your prayer you may suddenly realize that you too are anointed to stand up in some way, to get involved in some way, and to do your part in revealing the reign of God according to the particular ways you have

---

psalms. The yoke of liturgical prayer—high in predictability and low in drama—makes it "easy" and "light" for the Holy Spirit to pray through the disciplined and attentive soul. See Matthew 11:29–30, regarding Jesus' perfectly crafted yoke for growth in the spiritual life.

been gifted. Let the Holy Spirit pray through you! In the deepest sense even your prayer is vocational—not that you are asking God, "What do you want me to do?" Rather, your prayer becomes a response to God who already is urging you to participate in some way in the world's anguish and redemption. Vocationally, prayer comes down to this: You pray because Jesus is not yet finished praying to his Father.[32] Vocational prayer, amazingly, is not first and foremost about you.

What are these "inexpressible groanings" that St. Paul writes about? The late nineteenth century French Carmelite St. Thérèse of the Child Jesus once complained to her confessor, Père Pichon, that she was so worn out that all she could give God was a sigh. Père Pichon replied immediately: *Close to the Sacred Heart one sigh is very much; one sigh is sufficient for Him to open His Heart entirely to you. Dare, then, to complain again at having only a sigh!*[33] These are strong and instructive words on prayer from the pen of a spiritual master. What do they tell us? In prayer a sigh is not merely a sigh; it *is* the Holy Spirit, the Spirit of the risen Lord, interceding through you to move the heart of God.

Pray constantly, St. Paul urges.[34] Sigh, shed tears, be still, do what it honestly takes to give the Holy Spirit real freedom to pray through you. Maybe you think that your prayer does not matter all that much. Maybe you cannot understand your prayer, or cannot find words to adequately express what you mean to say, but God understands. The important thing here is not that you *also* understand, but that you remain faithful. Experiment, trust the fine-tuned promptings of the Holy Spirit, and pray accordingly. Present yourself faithfully to God, with a listening heart. Engaging in prayer, even—and especially—in

---

[32] This notion underlies my understanding of why the church prays the psalms of the Liturgy of the Hours. The psalms were Jesus' prayer language, and as long as any aspect of humankind or creation is in anguish, Jesus still intercedes with his Father—through us—on behalf of that suffering. See my essays "Listen for the Lord" and "Meditation on Three Words," in *Touching the Reign of God.*

[33] John Clarke, OCD, trans., *Letters of St. Thérèse of Lisieux, Volume II: 1890–1897* (Washington, DC: ICS Publications, 1988), 767.

[34] See 1 Thessalonians 5:17.

spiritually dry times, gives the Holy Spirit something to work with. We know this because "the one who searches hearts," St. Paul assures us, "knows what is the intention of the Spirit, because it intercedes for the holy ones according to God's will" (Romans 8:27).

I recommend you highlight this passage, Romans 8:26–27, in your Bible. Bookmark it, memorize it, let it shape your prayer and your spiritually intimate encounters with the living God. This passage will serve you well through all your life, through tough times, and in times when you feel completely confused, lost, and unable to pray as you think you ought.

God's Calling Seeks Relationship

This lifelong relationship with God—or, more intimately and more accurately, this *divine indwelling*—powered and shaped and directed by the Holy Spirit, is the vocational piece that is "confirmed" in Confirmation. God's calling is always about relationship—God with you, you with God, and God with the world through you. Your lifelong dynamic response to God's calling depends on the *quality* of your engagement in this divine-human relationship. Again, there is no magic here; nothing automatically happens just because you have been confirmed.

You can think of God's calling in this way: If your cell phone rings, it means that someone is trying to communicate with you. If you do not pick up the call, you cannot engage in conversation. Getting shuffled off to voicemail is not God's preferred way of engaging you in relationship. To be vocationally alive you have to *be here now,* ready to hear and pick up the call. God's calls come to you from every direction, often in the moments when you least expect them. God counts on each of us to be awake, aware, present to the moment.[35]

It's the same in all dimensions of life. You have to be present—not present and distracted, but present and paying attention to what is happening where you are right now—if you want to discover what God has in mind for your life. In a way we could say: No honest, authentic, living relationship with God? Then no way to hear God's calling. And without God's calling, you will never find a life that feels like it actually has your name on it. Sadly, some people in their forties, fifties, sixties, and beyond know all too well what this nameless life feels like.

God's calling may come as an interruption, but it will not be a burden. It may appear to others as an inconvenience, but it will be your surest source of joy. God's calling is so perfectly suited to *you* that you will realize one day that you cannot imagine *not* living this particular life, in these particular circumstances, doing this particular work in a wholehearted way. Jesus was speaking a vocational truth when he said: "Take my yoke upon you and learn from me, … [f]or my yoke is easy, and my burden light" (Matthew 11:29–30). The yoke, for many people in our culture today, is a symbol of unfreedom, and "burden" is another word for "bother." But the yoke which the Lord crafts uniquely for you makes carrying your share of the burden in revealing the reign of God a work of interior delight.[36]

---

[35] I recall a one-panel cartoon illustration, a contemporary rendering of Michelangelo's "Creation of Adam" fresco on the ceiling of the Sistine Chapel (Dan Piraro, Eugene [OR] *Register-Guard,* June 10, 2007). Here we see God, mighty Creator, reaching out with passionate creative intent toward the man—young, taut-muscled, reclining with a laptop strategically placed (complete with logo of an apple sporting a bite), cell phone to the ear, and free arm extended toward the Creator with hand raised as if to signal: "I'll be with you in a minute." A second example of the need to be ready for unexpected encounter with God comes in the story of the disciple who goes to the elder in search of Enlightenment. To achieve Enlightenment, the elder explains, "You must be here. The problem is that you are mostly somewhere else." See Joan Chittister, OSB, *Wisdom Distilled from the Daily: Living the Rule of St. Benedict Today* (San Francisco: HarperSanFrancisco, 1991), 201–202.

[36] A word of caution here: Some burdens we place on ourselves—the heavy boulders we put in our own buckets through indiscretion, through greed of one sort or another, or through a distortion of guilt. These are not the "burden" of the Gospel, to which Jesus refers, nor the Lord's yoke which amazingly leads to freedom to be our authentic self-in-God. Rather, quite by our own devices we

Be Who You Are

Vocationally, before God calls you to *do something,* God calls you to *be someone:* to be yourself—your authentic, real self, spiritually alive, pure of heart, morally uncompromised, wholehearted for the reign of God. Impossible to achieve? Actually, living a half life, spiritually asleep, morally compromised, and only half-hearted requires a whole lot more energy to keep you going, because then you are working *against* your God-given authentic nature and *against* the way you were built to be—whole and holy, fully alive in God.[37]

In your lifelong relationship with God, you never want God to be wondering where you are. You may be perfectly visible, but that is not the point. God is *restless for relationship*—for I and thou, for I-in-thou, for thou-in-Me. In the Book of Genesis we find God restless for relationship, for the enjoyment of friendship, with the man and the woman who were the very image of God.[38] After the fall, God walks through the garden in the breezy time of the day looking for them. But something is very wrong. The man and the woman have been tricked into believing that all that God had given them was somehow not enough. So they went for more. "Eat this fruit," the serpent cunningly urged, "and you will be like gods." But they already *were* the living, breathing image of the one God. *They became what they were never meant to be.* And God calls out, "Where are you?" (Genesis 3:9). Where, God wonders, are the man and the woman whom I created in my image? *I see you but I do not recognize you.*

The moral of this story remains powerful today. Be whom God has

---

have become skilled at crafting our own yoke which chafes and wears us down, and over time can lead to an infected and bitter spirit.

[37] Poet and author David Whyte observes that the antidote to the exhaustion of living a half life is wholeheartedness, a wisdom he gleaned in conversation with his friend Brother David Stendl-Rast. See David Whyte, *Crossing the Unknown Sea: Work as a Pilgrimage of Identity* (New York: Riverhead Books, 2001), 132.

[38] See Genesis 1:27.

created and anointed *you* to be: yourself, made in God's image, anointed for life, anointed for divine kinship and for an infinitely worthy purpose. Be recognizable by God by being your God-given self!

In the course of this lifelong intimate friendship which is yours, initiated in Baptism and sacramentally sealed in Confirmation, God will call you again and again—hopefully not because you are not listening, but because you are maturing and taking your relationship with Jesus and your unique role within his mission ever more seriously. Does this sound a little intimidating? Perhaps you recall Jesus' words to Peter after the resurrection: "[W]hen you were younger, you used to dress yourself and go where you wanted; but when you grow old, you will stretch out your hands, and someone else will dress you and lead you where you do not want to go" (John 21:18). Jesus was referring to the kind of death Peter would undergo to glorify God. Such a living—and a dying— is the ultimate expression of being conformed to Christ. St. Paul considered it an inescapable honor to undergo execution as his ultimate witness to his redeemer.

Chances are very good that you are not destined for a martyr's death, but in your life you will undergo experiences of the dying *and the rising,* of that paschal mystery which lie at the core of Christian faith. As you mature you will find yourself leaning deeper and deeper into the mystery of God, and experiencing loss and rejection and diminishment and perhaps great injustice, *and* by God's grace you will experience unexplainable, unmerited good. That's the dying and the rising of Christ Jesus, expressed now, one more time, in the circumstances of *your* life. You are one of God's anointed. You already have the capacity through the Holy Spirit to remain faithful and obedient in the moments of surrender to God's providence, so that Jesus can reveal the power of his resurrection in you and in those whose lives you touch.

How This Relationship Works

Every one of us stands vocationally in a "seismically active field," where the tremors of God's mighty yearning radiate outward constantly. God calls to each of us all the time: not always to "ultimate things," but in the circumstances of our lives God calls out patiently, urging us to take the next step, no matter how ordinary or obvious or even seemingly inconsequential it might be. Christian life is not about drama but about faithfulness and obedience—two lowly, overlooked, and undervalued spiritual qualities. How does this relationship, or dynamic intimate friendship, with God work? We can generally describe it this way:

- You might feel a tug in your heart to pray a word of love or yearning for God (remember—this is the Holy Spirit already praying God's love and yearning through you).[39]

- You may start to notice that you are becoming more deeply interested in certain studies, perhaps, or certain kinds of work; or you may find yourself drawn to and responding to certain kinds of situations, or immersing yourself among certain cultures or among certain groups who are marginalized in one way or another; and you may act on a hunch that you need to take this emerging interest seriously.

- You may volunteer for something, perhaps at first because you feel you have to, but interiorly something may shift, and you find yourself going back to do more, because over time you become unable to *not* engage in this work in this way.

These are indicators of a deepening vocational relationship with God. And this is how a mature, anointed, confirmed relationship with God grows. God always initiates—not by obvious and perfectly clear messages addressed to

---

[39] See my essay, "Meditation on Three Words," especially the section titled "In the Dark Space Before Dawn," in *Touching the Reign of God*, 50–55.

you, but through the things that interest you, the things that engage you, the things that incite you to live wholeheartedly in holiness and moral strength which in some way serves the good of others. God calls, you respond, and it's all "incarnational," in the richest Christian sense of the word. Your life in God is not just a "head" thing, or a "heart" thing, or merely a spiritual and private relationship. God at work in your life actually takes on flesh—*your* flesh—as you begin to participate more fully, more wholeheartedly, in your own life and in your world. You discover God in the hands-on moments, and in the moments of encounter with others. And you begin to realize that God has skin—*your* skin. In moments like this, you discover that you *are* the presence of the risen Christ for a hungry and hurting and hopeful world. This is what it means to be confirmed, to receive ongoing confirmation of God's calling of you, uniquely and personally, and to experience the Holy Spirit's movement in dynamic ways in your life.

Next we will look more closely at what it means to be Jesus' presence in our twenty-first century world.

Questions for Conversation

1.   What two or three points can I glean from this chapter?

2.   In what parts of my life does God have to ask: "Where are you?" Is it in my family relationships? my social relationships? my studies? my work? in my responsibilities to others? in my engagement in the larger community? Does God have to search for me in my prayer? in my recreation? my alone time? (Be specific; let details shed light on what needs your attention.)

3.   In what parts of my life do I feel deeply present to God? What am I doing in these situations? (Be specific.) Who benefits? What are the outcomes? What is this presence like for me? (Take time to describe and reflect on these experiences.)

4.   How would I describe my prayer life today? (Not what it's *like,* but what it actually *is,* what it actually consists of.) How is my prayer different today from what it was, say, six months ago? In what specific ways has it shifted focus, or tone, or intensity?

3

ANOINTED FOR A PURPOSE

You are the Presence of the Living Christ

It is not just your gifts that I discern: It is you yourself that I
encounter, you who cause me to share in your own being.

Père Teilhard de Chardin, SJ [40]

The most recent big leap forward in the life and trajectory of the church
came in the early 1960s, when the church awakened with new vigor to its
mission, its vocation, and its purpose: To turn, with the eyes of Love and the
clear voice of Justice, toward the world—this world which God still so loves.
This awakening came with the Second Vatican Council.[41] In the decades since

---

[40] Teilhard de Chardin, Pensées, in *Hymn of the Universe,* 10.

[41] I heard it said that the Council Fathers themselves did not understand the magnitude of the work
that they were undertaking, nor the discernments that they were making, so given were they to—or
so overcome by—the Holy Spirit. A fascinating insight into the groundbreaking work of the Council
Fathers can be found in Kathleen Hughes, RSCJ, *The Monk's Tale: A Biography of Godfrey
Diekmann, OSB* (Collegeville, MN: The Liturgical Press, 1991). Diekmann attended the Council as

then the church has moved from "waking up" to repositioning herself, in a world of ever-increasing moral complexity, for the arduous and urgent task of working, teaching, and advocating for the cause of life, and justice, and mercy, and peacemaking—all vital expressions of the reign of God. Guided by the inner reality and deep implications of the Incarnation, the church in today's world presses forward and vigorously strives to defend an inviolable space of dignity, hope, and rightful participation—for humankind and indeed for all of creation—in the redeemed order of the reign of God in the risen Christ.[42]

Pentecost Today

The next big leap forward in the life and trajectory of the church will come when you and I and our fellow believers embrace Pentecost and the deeper reality of our sacramental anointing in a radically new way. Following his resurrection the risen Lord appeared to the Eleven, bestowed upon them his gift of peace, and breathed his Spirit onto them.[43] And from that moment on their lives could never be the same—as attested to in the accounts of the early church. These followers, foolish enough (by human measure) to give their lives to this Jesus who was crucified and raised from the dead, were human beings—mere mortals—walking around with the Spirit of God burning like unquenchable fire within them, the Spirit of the risen Christ breathing through them and outward to the world.

In addition to this post-Resurrection account of the gifting of the Holy Spirit, found in the Gospel of St. John, the Acts of the Apostles offers us another account, this time of Pentecost, when again the Spirit was given, here as tongues

---

an expert consultant and took leadership in drafting the *Constitution on the Sacred Liturgy,* the first major document to emerge from the Council.

[42] See *Pastoral Constitution on the Church in the Modern World,* in Austin Flannery, OP, gen. ed., *Vatican Council II, Volume 1: The Conciliar and Post Conciliar Documents* (Northport, NY: Costello Publishing, 1975, 1998), 903–1001.

[43] See John 20:21–22.

of fire which came to rest on each of the Apostles.[44] Each received a very personal and undeniable empowerment, a consecration, a personal anointing in the Holy Spirit—not so that the Apostles could "be like" Jesus, but so that they could actually stand with full authority in his place, breathing his breath, speaking his words, and confidently doing his works—the work of revealing the reign of God.

In our twenty-first century—far removed in time from that Spirit-drenched experience of the early church—we have somehow settled into the comfortable and mistaken belief that the Christian way of life is to *be like* Jesus. But such thinking misses the point and sadly reveals an impoverished understanding of the sacramental anointing of Christian life. Being *like* Jesus falls short of radical participation in the authority and power of God's mission entrusted to us in sacrament. Being *like* Jesus can never be enough. The real purpose of your sacramental anointing—in Baptism and more completely in Confirmation—is this: To empower you to stand, with authority, humility, and faith, *in the place of Jesus* in order to do the works of God, and to reveal the reign of God in this time and place, in these particular circumstances. So the appropriate—or vocationally relevant—question becomes: "Lord, how are *you* desiring to act *through me* in this situation, in these circumstances, in this time and place?" The focus here shifts from "me doing the right thing" to the Spirit of the living Christ accomplishing God's willing through me.[45]

In the Gospel of St. John we hear Jesus speak a phrase that seems startling and even counter to what we understand of him. Jesus says to his

---

[44] See Acts 2:1–4.

[45] I think of a friend whose young adult daughter was given psychosis inducing drugs. While my friend is committed to journeying with her daughter through the state's mental health system, she has awakened to a deeper vocational reality—that she now is called upon to stand in the place of Jesus, providing compassionate care, stability, healing, and encouragement to her suffering daughter, and to defend a space of dignity and justice through advocacy for her daughter and for others like her—labeled "schizophrenic," heavily medicated, voiceless, and trapped in "the treatment machine." Says my friend, "I would not have chosen this path for my life, but I draw strength in believing that God has chosen me to be the mother of this child in her space of extreme spiritual suffering, and to be God's voice of justice and advocacy."

disciples, "[W]hoever believes in me will do the works that I do, and *will do greater ones than these,* because I am going to the Father" (John 14:12, emphasis added). Just as Jesus' adversaries wondered who he took himself to be, so we might wonder who Jesus takes *us* to be. What does Jesus mean when he says that we will do works even greater than his? The Gospels do not say that Jesus healed everyone; he healed a few people—many, even—in a very small geographic area of the world. He fed the multitudes, but he did not remove hunger and poverty from the face of the earth. Indeed, he reminded his followers that the poor would always be drawn to them,[46] perhaps because the poor would somehow know that these followers of Jesus could be counted on to generously defend a space and a portion of good for them.

If you look at the anguished condition of our world today, if you look at the wars and the habit of war, the disasters and tragedies and the trail of suffering they leave in their wake; if you look at the social and personal injustices that have disfigured the human spirit for generations, you realize that Jesus' life, death, and resurrection did not suddenly right all the wrongs of the world. He came to show us how the works of love, of justice, of mercy, and of peacemaking are done. "As I have done, so you must do," he told his closest followers on the night before his arrest.[47] How sobering, this intimate identification with the Lord whose nail scars proved how deeply God is invested in restoring this world to its original grace, beauty, and purpose. This intimate identification with the crucified and risen Lord is the necessary starting point of vocational awakening.

"As the Father has sent me, *so I send you,*" Jesus says (John 20:21, emphasis added). These words of commissioning are as direct and intentional for us today as they were for that earliest core group of Jesus' followers. In receiving the Holy Spirit in Baptism and being sealed in that same Spirit in Confirmation, we are no longer *like* Jesus. None of us has any excuses behind

---

[46] See John 12:8.

[47] See John 13:15.

which we can hide. Our anointing *exposes* us to God's designs, and our participation in those designs is not optional. Jesus does not say "imitate me" but, in essence he says, "stand in my place, with my authority, and with the humility and complete trust in my Father which has shaped *my* life."

These words of commissioning give power and life to your sacramental anointing. Let's take a closer look at these words.

Authority, Humility, Radical Trust in God

Authority is a power to act that does not start with any of us but comes from a far greater source. Authority, properly understood, is given, bestowed, received. We regard God as the "ultimate authority," and rightly so, as God is the *author* or source of all life.[48] Real authority can never be greedily snatched but, rather, is entrusted to one to rightly give commands ordered toward the good of others, to govern or exercise stewardship prudently, to make decisions, to take action on behalf of another or on behalf of an entity much larger than oneself. *Real authority flows from God and always serves the good.* Real authority opens the doors of the reign of God, as witnessed in the life, mission, death, and resurrection of Jesus. Our world is full of people who snatch so-called "authority" to serve their own purposes and to dominate, or to deny the freedom and dignity of others. But that is not authority; that is license, snatching the holy fire of divine intent for unholy purposes, expressing a reckless moral disregard for the well-being of others, and bearing results that are dead to the reign of God.

---

[48] God's ultimate authority is acknowledged in praying the very simple phrase, "All life, all holiness comes from you" in Eucharistic Prayer III of *The Roman Missal: Second Edition* (New York: Catholic Book Publishing, 1985)—or more extensively worded in *The Roman Missal: Third Edition* (Washington, DC: ICEL, 2010) "for through your Son our Lord Jesus Christ, by the power and working of the Holy Spirit, you give life to all things and make them holy."

Jesus, however, is described in the Gospels as *having* authority,[49] *teaching* with authority,[50] and *sharing* authority.[51] The risen Lord makes an astonishing declaration when he extends his divine authority to his core followers: "Whose sins *you* forgive are forgiven them" (John 20:23, emphasis added). Now the risen Lord hands on to the Apostles the theological scandal for which he himself was earlier chastised and later executed.[52]

Jesus is very clear about two things, both of which are important to understand and take deeply to heart: First, Jesus' authority *is* the Holy Spirit and the activity of the Holy Spirit; it is an active and effective authority bestowed by his Father in his earthly mission, and which Jesus has enjoyed always with his Father.[53] Second, this authority is always used for others' good, revealing the reign of God in particular circumstances.[54]

What does this authority of the living Christ mean for you? If you are baptized and are breathing at this moment, that very same Spirit—that very

---

[49] See Mark 11:27–33, where the scribes and elders question the source of Jesus' authority. See also Matthew 21:23–27; Luke 20:1–8.

[50] See Matthew 7:29, at the end of Jesus' great inaugural teaching, where people were "astonished at his teaching, for he taught them as one having authority, and not as their scribes." See also Mark 1:22 and Luke 4:32 for similar accounts.

[51] See Matthew 10:1, the commissioning of the Twelve (also in Mark 3:13–15). See also John 20:21–23, where the risen Lord says to his closest band of followers: "Peace be with you. As the Father has sent me, so I send you." Then, in the act of conferring his divine authority, he breathes on them and says: "Receive the holy Spirit"—the same "Advocate, the holy Spirit," promised by Jesus, who "will teach you everything and remind you of all that [I] told you" (see John 14:26).

[52] See Mark 2:7, where the scribes murmured, "Why does this man speak that way? ... Who but God alone can forgive sins?" See also Mark 14:55–64, where Jesus' trial revolves around the question of his divine authority.

[53] See John 10:30: "The Father and I are one," echoing the opening line of St. John's Gospel: "In the beginning was the Word, / and the Word was with God, / and the Word was God" (John 1:1). See also John 12:44–45: "Whoever believes in me believes not only in me but also in the one who sent me, and whoever sees me sees the one who sent me"; and 14:9–10, where Jesus says to Philip, "How can you say, 'Show us the Father'? Do you not believe that I am in the Father and the Father is in me?" This theme of divine communion, the indwelling of Father and Son inseparable in the Holy Spirit, runs throughout St. John's Gospel. By extension, the author of this Gospel unavoidably insists on the divine-human indwelling, expressed most ardently in Jesus' prayer on the night before he died (see John 17).

[54] In speaking of his mission in terms of shepherd and sheep gate, Jesus says simply: "I came so that they may have life and have it more abundantly." In metaphors of hunger (food) and thirst (drink), Jesus likewise expresses his divine authority in service to the good of others (see John 4:13–14; 6:35; 7:37–38).

same divine authority—resides within you. This is the scandal of Christian faith, that you and I walk this Earth with the Spirit of the living Christ in us. We have been gifted to reveal the truly miraculous and transformative power of our sacramental anointing which initiates and affirms us in our participation in God's loving work of redemption.

This understanding of divine authority leads us to our second word: *humility.* You are anointed not only in God's *authority* to participate in this work of redemption. You are anointed in God's *humility.* This phrase—*God's humility*—may sound startling. If anyone should be exempt from humility, surely it would be God. Yet Jesus—God incarnate—did not deem equality with his Father as a "card" he could play at will.[55] God, in the person of Jesus, is utterly self-effacing. When St. Paul insists of Christians an *attitude* of divine humility, he puts forward an attitude which stands in stark contrast to what we understand by "attitude" today, which boasts, "It's all about me."[56] In the mighty work of redemption God's motto expressing divine humility could be: "It's not about me; it's all about you."

In Jesus' inaugural sermon on the mount, his teaching was intended to be deeply formative on the spiritual dimensions of personal life and relationship with others. He elevated the interior posture of humility to a spiritual strength: "Blessed are the poor in spirit, … Blessed are they who mourn, … Blessed are the meek, … Blessed are they who hunger and thirst for righteousness, … the merciful, … the clean of heart" (Matthew 5:3–8). This interior posture of humility in fact is necessary to strengthen one to be the peacemaker in the mist of conflict, the one able to withstand persecution for the sake of righteousness and not run away.[57] Humility, we discover, becomes not a sign of weakness but

---

[55] See Philippians 2:6–7. The lead-in phrase (v. 5) to this canticle of the early church says, in essence, *Your attitude must be Christ's.* St. Paul minces no words in his exhortation to us to become our fullest self-in-Christ by conforming ourselves to his humility.

[56] I recently heard someone speak a "bumper sticker" phrase: "I have an attitude, and I use it." But imagine, I thought, the quite opposite phrase, which one might speak interiorly: "I have humility, and I use it."

[57] See Matthew 5:9–12.

a spiritual armor that protects the authentic self-in-God and defends against the hubris of an arrogant spirit.

Jesus had a heart for the ones of little or no account, the ones you and I might pass by and never notice. He had a heart for those who bore the costly burden of labor, the ones who would never gain traction on the road to success. And he kept coming back to them, encouraging them in the midst of their wretched circumstances. He did not extract them from their humble state in life but showed them how to labor in that state *with grace:* "Take *my* yoke upon you and learn from me," he says, "for I am meek and humble of heart. … For *my* yoke is easy, and *my* burden is light" (Matthew 11:29–30, emphasis added). If you chafe against your lot in life, the Master seems to say, the yoke of your circumstances will chafe against you. But if you harness yourself with the yoke of true humility ("my yoke"), you will find relief from the burden. "Observe me well," Jesus seems to say, "for by my living and my dying I will show you what true humility looks like, and you will see the fruit it bears."

To what lengths of humility would God go to win our hearts? We have only to look at Jesus on the cross, obediently crossing the threshold from humility to outright humiliation. Jesus was a fool for Love, God's Fool revealing an unbounded divine and foolish love for the likes of you and me. St. Paul writes of God's astonishing humility: "Indeed, only with difficulty does one die for a just person. … But God proves his love for us in that while we were still sinners Christ died for us" (Romans 5:7–8). By today's standards, in a world where greed, supposedly, is good, Jesus has "Fool" chiseled into his flesh, and he bears his scars with redeeming grace and dignity.

That same humble, self-effacing Spirit of the risen Lord is in each of us, ready to express through our actions, our presence, and our attitude God's foolish love for those whose lives we touch. God is not finished loving the world, and therefore each of us has been anointed into the company of humble, servant-hearted holy fools in service to God's life-giving, healing, redeeming love. Tellingly, when Jesus describes himself as "meek and humble of heart" (Matthew 11:29), he seems to say *I am of the earth,* as though playing on the root of the word "humble"—*humus,* or *of the earth.* In essence he says, "I, your Lord, am not too good for you." In an act of humility so startling that it rattled Peter, Jesus washes the feet of his disciples on their last evening together.[58] This *attitude* of humility and service to others is the "mind of Christ" which St. Paul urges in each of us.[59]

Jesus' life and works show us how God's authority in us and our humility toward others is essential to authentic life in the Holy Spirit. But one element remains, which gives power to authority and life to humility. That element is *faith*—or what I call *radical trust in God.* This is not merely a faith that says, "Yes, I believe in God; God will not abandon me, God will see me through." I am speaking here of faith which is resolute, unflinching, compelling and big and bold, liberating you to actually live at the courageous threshold rather than at the safe center of life. I am speaking of an absolute and radical trust that your anointing in the Spirit of the living Christ is *meant* to be effective, and serving a purpose beyond what you can imagine. I am speaking of an animating force that unshackles you from doubt, hesitation, or fear, freeing you to lean completely into Jesus, and to be present and clear and bold with his own presence and clarity and boldness, fully alive with his divine imagination and initiative, in the part of this twenty-first century world that you personally inhabit and touch.

This dynamic faith, or absolute trust in God and in the effective power of your anointing, *sets you free* to rise up, step forth with grace, and be your authentic self-in-God—not diminished or half-hearted or fearful, but to be the

---

[58] See John 13:3–7. The ritual nature of this footwashing puts the focus not on the practical work of bathing another person (see vv. 8–10 where Peter resists, then tells the Lord to wash his hands and head as well as his feet), but on expression of humility in servitude (see v. 14, "If I, therefore, the master and teacher, have washed your feet, you ought to wash one another's feet").

[59] See Philippians 2:5.

self whom God sees and knows and has long, long desired. Radical trust in God isn't about calculating which career will assure you the most "climb," or which job will provide the best pension, or which potential marriage partner will be "just right" for you (assuming you could know what "just right" would look like). Radical trust in God is about listening to God faithfully, where you are right now, developing the habit of deep listening, and noticing how the Holy Spirit already is at work in the various circumstances of your life, prompting you to see, observe, feel, and respond to the concerns of your world according to the ways you have been gifted by God.

Radical trust in God sets you free, over time, to live every dimension of your life boldly for God, and to stand "with all your heart, with all your soul, with all your mind, and with all your strength" in the place of Jesus.[60] Your absolute trust in God enables you to get out of the boat willingly in the midst of the storm because Jesus, with eyes full of love and encouragement, beckons you to join him in the place of seeming uncertainty and obvious impossibility, perhaps for no other reason than to reveal to you a divine "new normal."[61] Indeed, your absolute trust in God gives the Holy Spirit capacity to accomplish "greater things than these" through you.[62]

So there is nothing passive or fleeting or small about this anointing which you have received in Confirmation. This anointing is a sharing in the fire at the core of God's heart, now leaping to life within you. But nothing happens "automatically" just because you "went through Confirmation." Like every other dimension of Christian life, this sacrament requires your lifelong courageous and loving Yes, and your wholehearted partnership with the Holy Spirit, in order for this sacramental relationship to mature and bear fruit over the course of your life.

---

[60] Mark 12:30. This "greatest commandment" is not merely our means to "winning heaven" but is the essential means by which Jesus' work of redemption is carried out on the earthly plane throughout the ages.

[61] See Matthew 14:22–29. Peter was not yet ready for "the new normal" (see v. 30).

[62] See John 14:12.

What is required of you is faithfulness, being present daily, and listening attentively with the ear of the heart to God's Word and to the still small voice of the Holy Spirit. All God asks of you is to be present and engaged in the demands, the routine, and the commitments of your life, and to share wholeheartedly in the life and missional work of the Christian community. No matter your age or your state in life, you are a full partner now with the Holy Spirit in the work of revealing the reign of God and achieving your wholeness and holiness in God. That is your real vocation, your life's work. What you do for a living hopefully will be a fitting expression of who you are in God, and will be a means of achieving completeness of your personhood. You are anointed for a purpose, and God's purposes ultimately will be fulfilled.[63]

A Closer Look at Anointing

To *anoint,* to be *anointed:* What does this mean? We usually think of this word *anointing* in its spiritual context. But what does this word mean as human activity and therefore as a dimension of Christian sacramental life? The root of the word *anoint* means to smear in, as an ointment or oil; to bring about healing (as the Good Samaritan used oil to dress the man's open wounds); to limber up muscles and joints by use of oil (as Greek athletes would do before sporting competitions, and as warriors would do to prepare for battle). In Israel, kings were lavishly anointed with oil, by which they were set apart, or consecrated, for the sacred duty of leading God's people.[64]

The word *anoint,* including its various forms (anointed, anointing) appears one hundred forty-three times in the Old Testament, and nineteen times

---

[63] At the darkest period of his life Blessed John Henry Cardinal Newman wrote, "God has determined, unless I interfere with His plan, that I should reach that which will be my greatest happiness. He looks on me individually, He calls me by my name, He knows what I can do, what I can best be, what is my greatest happiness, and He means to give it to me." From Meditation 299 (1), "Hope in God-Creator," March 6, 1848, http://www.newmanreader.org/works/meditations/meditations9.html#doctrine1 (accessed July 15, 2011).

[64] See 1 Samuel 16:12–13 and 2 Samuel 5:3 regarding the anointing of David.

in the New Testament.[65] The Psalms offer perhaps the most poetic and consoling images of divine anointing for spiritual strength. Psalm 23 (at v. 5) extols God who "set[s] a table before me / as my enemies watch; / You anoint my head with oil; / my cup overflows." In Psalm 92 the Psalmist declares the protective strength of divine anointing for spiritual battle: "To me you give the wild-ox's strength; / you anoint me with the purest oil. / My eyes looked in triumph on my foes; / my ears heard gladly of their fall."[66]

In the Gospels, the term *Christ* has a Greek root meaning "the Anointed one of God."[67] Jesus, the Christ, the Messiah, was anointed and sent by God for a mission. In his inaugural teaching in the synagogue, recounted in the Gospel of St. Luke, Jesus reads the passage from the scroll of the prophet Isaiah: "'The Spirit of the Lord is upon me, / because he has anointed me / to bring glad tidings to the poor. ...' Rolling up the scroll, he ... said to them, 'Today this scripture passage is fulfilled in your hearing.'"[68] This passage from St. Luke's Gospel illustrates another expression of the term *anointed:* to be consecrated or set aside for a divine purpose or a sacred mission. While Jesus was baptized with the baptism of John,[69] we do not find scriptural evidence of an actual anointing of Jesus as in smearing with the kingly oils of the Old Testament or with sacred chrism.[70] The Synoptic accounts[71] of Jesus' baptism record that "a voice came from the heavens, saying, 'This is my beloved Son, with whom I am

---

[65] Strong, *Concordance,* s.vv. "Anoint," "Anointed," "Anointing."

[66] Psalm 92:11–12 (stanza 4 of the Grail translation). See *Christian Prayer: The Liturgy of the Hours* (New York: Catholic Book Publishing, 1976). Psalm texts except Psalm 95 from *The Psalms: A New Translation* (England: The Grail, 1963), 846.

[67] See Mark 8:29; John 4:25. In the *NAB* the word is "Messiah," a word with a Hebrew and Aramaic root meaning "anointed."

[68] See Luke 4:16–21, especially vv. 18–21.

[69] See Matthew 3:13–17; Mark 1:9–11; Luke 3:21–22; John 1:32–33.

[70] In Acts 4:27 the early community prayed to God, recalling "your holy servant Jesus whom you anointed." In Acts 10:38 we read: "God anointed Jesus of Nazareth with the holy Spirit and power."

[71] The term *synoptic* essentially means "seen through the same lens" or "viewed in the same way." This term has been applied to the Gospels of Matthew, Mark, and Luke. Much core material, coming from St. Mark's early Gospel, is found paralleled in the later Gospels of St. Matthew and St. Luke.

well pleased'" (Matthew 3:17).[72]

In the church's sacramental expression of this divine consecration each of us has been anointed and sent by God to share in this divine mission: to enable every person to encounter the living Christ and to restore all dimensions of human society and all of creation to right relationship in God, as Jesus proclaimed in the passage from Isaiah and appropriated as his own mission. As long as this world continues, God will be on this mission, and will continue to anoint people like you and me in Christ Jesus, in the power of the Holy Spirit, in order to give flesh and spirit and life to the particulars of redemption in this time and place. Each of us is anointed for a unique work of healing, restoration, and love in this world; each of us has been anointed, consecrated, set apart by God's design, to participate in this holy mission of redemption, according to the ways God has been pleased to gift us.

What This Anointing Looks Like

The actual physical anointing with sacred chrism administered in Confirmation takes but a moment, a small portion of a minute, as the bishop smears the fragrant ointment on the forehead of the one being confirmed. This anointing, accompanied by the laying on of hands, "is rightly recognized by the Catholic tradition as the origin of the sacrament of Confirmation, which in a certain way perpetuates the grace of Pentecost in the Church."[73] But what is the *ongoing experience* of this sacramental anointing? What does this consist of? How might we describe it?

At the core of this ongoing sacramental anointing is a *remembering* which is more than merely recalling something that happened in the past.

---

[72] See also Mark 1:11 and Luke 3:22: "You are my beloved Son; with you I am well pleased." The phrasing in these two accounts is conversational, rather than descriptive as in St. Matthew's account.
[73] *CCC* 1288.

Liturgically and sacramentally when we speak of *remembering* we speak of a living and active calling to mind and to heart which renders an act of the past a living reality in the present as we surrender to its redemptive claim upon us. This quality of remembering lies at the heart of our experience of Eucharist. In the institution narrative, we hear the words: *Do this in memory of me,* and we give ourselves over to the living truth of these words and these gestures. We encounter, in the humble elements of bread and wine, the living presence of the risen Lord. So also with the remembering of our anointing in Confirmation. When we give ourselves over faithfully to the deeper and enduring reality of this anointing, we encounter once again the power of that anointing in new and vocationally-charged ways.

In my own experience, what I encounter in this ongoing sacramental anointing in the Holy Spirit is a daily surrender to God's perfect willing for my life. This is no mere quick mental exercise. Rather, I have to personally present myself before God in prayer each morning; look at my day, my plans, and my commitments through the lens of the Gospel, and intentionally place myself in service to the Lord. In essence I say to the Lord: "I am yours. I am at your service. I stand anointed for your purposes this day." The key requirement here is the intentionality. You will find that this daily anointing gives life and spark, meaning and direction, to this living relationship between self, God, and the world.[74] It is not that you continually receive the anointing but that you grow deeper into the anointing you have already received.

We are all equally lavishly anointed, each of us receiving a full portion of the Holy Spirit. God has absolutely no interest in generously anointing one person and holding back with another. *The great saints were not more anointed*

---

[74] For me the clearest demonstration of this ongoing anointing for service to the Lord came not too long ago. After five years of uphill climb, I decided that I no longer wanted to be the president and CEO of my company. So I brought in a new management team—the Holy Trinity: Father as the visionary leader, Son as chief operations officer to whom I report, and Holy Spirit, the animator of the mission. At first I laughed at the thought. Then I realized that this "corporate arrangement" was the only way I could make sense of my efforts. Ever since then, I have been presenting myself to the Lord each morning for the day's assignments, assured of the anointing to carry them out.

than you or me. Those called to priesthood or religious life are richly anointed, as are those who may live quite ordinary or hidden yet faithful and fruitful lives. *How* you work with that anointing reveals the degree of spiritual freedom, or sometimes unfreedom, you bring to your work of becoming your authentic self-in-God.

If you have a habit of laziness, or if you persistently submerge yourself in constant noise and distractions and restless busyness, or if you bounce from one excuse for nonengagement to the next, you will find that you are resisting the full effects of your anointing. The quality of your engagement in this interior freedom of anointing in the Holy Spirit is up to you. You can intentionally choose God at every turn and choose to continually expand your capacity for God,[75] or you can choose your own agenda, run away from your anointing, cling to whatever promises to buffer you from the reality of your calling, and wonder why your life feels so empty.[76]

Immersing yourself ever more deeply in the anointing of the Holy Spirit is a lifelong activity, reflected in your ever-deepening engagement in key relationships, in study, and in meaningful and fulfilling work. In the moment of Confirmation you are anointed both physically and, in a spiritual way, indelibly. Your spiritual work over the course of your life is to continually open yourself more fully to the mystery and full effect of that anointing. This opening of heart and mind and spirit and imagination is intentional, something you commit to, not as one among many commitments but as the one core commitment that gives life and breath, meaning and direction, to all the other dimensions of your life. With disciplined practice over time you learn to intentionally orient your heart and soul and mind and strength[77] toward this lifelong anointing in the Holy Spirit. And with disciplined practiced, you learn to commit your plans, your

---

[75] See Joshua 24:15, "[D]ecide today whom you will serve."

[76] See Mark 10:17–22, where the rich man who wanted to inherit eternal life could not part with his possessions.

[77] See Mark 12:30.

discernments and your actions, your priorities, your attitude, and your understanding to the power of this anointing.

This discipline of taking your relationship with Jesus more seriously because of this deeper anointing is the exact opposite of the way some people may experience Confirmation—as "graduation from church." For younger people, sometimes this "graduation" and leave-taking can happen abruptly, as soon as they "get through Confirmation." But for some of us who are older, our "graduation from church" may have taken longer, or been less obvious. Perhaps in our forties or fifties we conclude that the world's sophistication and more practical approach to morally complex issues just does not intersect with what the church teaches. Or maybe in our sixties or seventies we begin to wonder where decades of obedience—which may have felt more like compliance—has gotten us. Given today's social and moral pressures, how do you get to the point where living with the Holy Spirit as the animating force at the center of your life becomes the norm? Such commitment does not spring up overnight. It requires, in fact, putting your hand to the plow and not looking back.[78]

Three Helpful Steps

You *can* develop the practice of living with the Holy Spirit as the animating force at the center of your life. And it is in fact a *practice,* requiring your ongoing wholehearted commitment. These three steps will help you.

First, commit to *active participation in the life and prayer of the Christian community.* No matter the stage of life in which you find yourself, your active participation is a discipline, a practice, and a commitment. Be active in your parish. If you do not have a parish, find one. Enroll, sign up, commit.[79]

---

[78] See Luke 9:62.

[79] I once heard of a person who asked, "I wonder if my name is in the Book of Life." A friend replied, *"Did you sign up?"*

Take your place at the table; get known, even if you are young, even if you are old; even if you are single, widowed, or divorced; even if you are feeling insignificant, marginalized, or socially awkward. When you are feeling weak or wavering, the faith of the Christian community will sustain you. When you are feeling strong and engaged, you will be strength and inspiration for those who feel adrift. This is the way the Spirit-led Christian community works. Find the faith-keepers in the parish, the ones who stand close enough to the sacred Fire to emit sparks, the ones burnished by life lived in the crucible of Love. Get to know them, and let them get to know you.

Second, *commit to a regular prayer life*—not as an add-on but as the engine that allows every dimension of your life to flow vocationally from God and to return fruitfully to God.[80] If your life is too busy for prayer, get rid of some of the busyness; let go the distractions that add up to a lot of lost time with nothing to show at the end of the day. If you are too busy doing God's work, then you cannot afford to *not* pray. No matter your age, no matter your role or gender or your state or stage in life, a regular prayer life for you is as necessary for your interior survival as breathing is for the body. This statement is not an exaggeration but the simple truth. What matters is not the accumulation of time spent in prayer, or the volume of prayers said, but the quality of honest, authentic relationship with the Lord. Spiritual intimacy with God, with the living Christ, demands time, intentionality, and real presence.

Third, *be awake to your life, your relationships, your commitments, your world:* Act in all circumstances with the mind and heart of Jesus—whether you are listening to the daily news, encountering a neighbor in need, or sorting through a complicated situation at work. Again, this is a discipline practiced over time, a commitment of faith, and a commitment to faithfulness. No one else

---

[80] A "Vocation Wheel" which illustrates how the many dimensions of your life currently do—or do not—flow from and return to God at the center is available as a pdf file at http://www.awakening vocations.com/welcome.html. This circular diagram offers a more workable model of relationship with God than the linear model of God "at the top" or "first," with family, work, and other commitments "farther down the ladder." The encircled model, with its outward–inward flow, is akin to the systolic–diastolic action of the heart.

can stand in your place to be the presence of the living Christ in these particular situations. No one else can fulfill what God uniquely desires *you* to do and to be for others, *these* particular others, at *this* particular place and time.

Relationship with God, in the Holy Spirit, is not rocket science. Nor does it require great wealth or exceptional intelligence. It does require faithfulness and obedience, humility and trust, and a steadfast commitment to deepen this relationship. While relationship with God may be simple, it will not always be easy—as Jesus would be the first to attest.

Standing in Jesus' Place in a Twenty-first Century World

It is not at all by chance that you were born when you were, into your particular family system, into your particular town, in one particular region of the country or the world, and coming to maturity in the complex moral and cultural environment of the late twentieth and early twenty-first centuries. What does all of this mean? We do not know for sure, but as you take greater responsibility for your relationship with Jesus, and as you mature in your life, you will get glimpses of insight into God's love and provision for your life and for those whom God touches through you. Those glimpses of insight will continue for as long as you live. God is an amazing mystery of infinite and inescapable love, and has chosen you in unique ways as a channel for that love. This we know for certain.

What is this twenty-first century world turning out to be? It defines itself more clearly each week. Just listen to the news, or watch TV, or notice what is going on around you, in your own town. Life as it once was, or as we imagined or expected it to be, is over, and we move forward into what we do not yet know and cannot yet imagine. Our twenty-first century world seems poised at the tipping point, defined by imbalances of unimaginable proportions— economically, socially, environmentally, and morally. We sow seeds of breathtaking research in science and medicine, and reap a briar patch of ethical questions. The pursuit of peace and justice, and preservation of dignity of the human person and of all creation can be regarded as weak posturing, endangering our safety or curbing our liberties, inconvenient to our lifestyle, impossible to achieve, and a hindrance to progress and profits. We have become beholden to a phantom economy which is far removed from real labor and honest stewardship of Earth's natural wealth. Is this world as we encounter it today a good picture of the reign of God? This question confronts each of us daily, and demands our honest, moral, imaginative, and wholehearted response.

In his parables and his teachings, Jesus continually pointed to what the reign of God is like. In St. Matthew's Gospel Jesus says that the reign of God is like a man who sows good seed in his field;[81] like yeast which a woman mixes with three measures of wheat flour;[82] like treasure buried in a field;[83] like a merchant in search of fine pearls;[84] like a fishing net cast broadly into the sea.[85] These are very ordinary images of people laboring, people like you and me engaged in very ordinary things, simple actions in the line of commerce, of day-to-day work, or household activity.

What good seed is yours to sow? How do you mix the Holy Spirit into what you are creating? What is the buried treasure, the pearl, for which you will gladly sell everything you have in order to purchase? How broadly and how boldly are you willing to cast your net? The guiding question here is: How broadly and boldly was this man Jesus willing to cast *his* net? You stand in Jesus' place in your twenty-first century world. Observe Jesus closely, learn from the Master. Revealing the reign of God in your place and time is your immediate concern.

---

[81] See Matthew 13:24.

[82] See Matthew 13:33.

[83] See Matthew 13:44.

[84] See Matthew 13:45.

[85] See Matthew 13:47.

Anointed for Priestly, Prophetic, Kingly Work

Many voices today insist that the pursuit of peace and justice, and preservation of dignity of the human person and of all creation is misguided, ineffective, not worth the bother, a project too big, too costly, too late. Besides, the facts are not all in; we may be wrong. The problem we think we need to fix may be exaggerated. Maybe the pursuit of peace and justice, and preservation of the dignity of the human person and of all creation is not even our concern, or maybe it should be someone else's. Many voices today may try to convince us that we are trying too hard, that we care too much, that injustices and inequities are just a part of life, so we should probably just get used to it and get on with our lives.

But the reign of God shows us otherwise, as Jesus' life, death, and resurrection have made clear. You were not baptized and anointed into service of the Land of the Upside Down, where perversion of what is lovely and good rules the day. No, you were baptized and anointed into service of the Land of the Rightside Up, into the reign of God, where a living passion for moral right and justice, compassion, dignity, and the divine spark of imagination becomes the path to holiness of life and a means of redeemed wholeness for the world.[86]

You have been anointed, consecrated, set apart as Jesus was, to get your heart mixed up with the world's anguish—not to become destroyed by the world's anguish but to make of it, as Jesus did, a complete offering to his Father's mercy and the worthy subject of redemption. You have been anointed to intercede as Jesus did, as the saints do, for the life of the world. You *are* one

---

[86] I take these images, the Land of the Upside Down and the Land of the Rightside Up, from my reflection on the account of Jesus cleansing the temple—an event significant enough to appear in all four Gospels (Matthew 21:12–13; Mark 11:15–18; Luke 19:45–46; and John 2:14–16). Jesus' work was not to destroy the existing order but to cleanse and restore it to its original loveliness and purpose, as found in the original garden in Genesis 1. I take it as not by chance that the risen Lord first appears in "the garden," mistaken as "the gardener" (see John 20:15).

of the saints. In Baptism you have been anointed as *priest,* as the prophet Joel says, to stand in the breach where anguish dwells and, in prayer and supplication, to "weep, / And say, 'Spare, O LORD, your people, / and make not your heritage a reproach.'"[87] In Christ Jesus you hold the authority to intercede for fullness of redemption of the world's anguish—especially those parts of the world which you touch, or which touch you in some way. This wholehearted intercession is your *priestly* work now.

In Baptism and Confirmation you have been anointed, consecrated, set apart as Jesus was, to know the heart and loving intention of the Father, and to engage in your world accordingly. Jesus did not heal everyone; he healed a few, so that we could see how it's done. He did not encounter everyone with his words of forgiveness; he encountered a few, so that we could see how it's done. He did not right every wrong and counter every hypocrisy, but he did it enough to show us how it's done. He lived once, died once, and by God's favor was raised to new life once, to show us how it's done.

Because you are anointed into Jesus, the living Christ, it is vital, imperative, that you read the Gospels, study them prayerfully and intently. Pay attention to what the Teacher is teaching you; reflect on your own experience and the circumstances of your life. Look around you, wake up, pay attention, and notice, really notice, what in the world is going on. Do not simply wonder, "What would Jesus do?" Stand up in Jesus' place, be bold in the Holy Spirit, and act with faithfulness, obedience, humility, and uncompromised trust in the living God. Let Jesus' passion for his Father's redemptive mission become a living flame in you. Let the divine sparks fly.

Live as though you are *anointed* in the power of the Holy Spirit— because you are. Read the news daily for what it is—the ongoing story of the world's anguish and hope, and read the larger signs of the times through the lens

---

[87] Joel 2:17. See also Joel 1:13–14 which describes the priestly work of intercession: "Gird yourselves and weep, O priests! / wail, O ministers of the altar! / ... Gather the elders, / ... [i]nto the house of the Lord, your God, / and cry to the Lord!"

of the Gospel.[88] Listen carefully and observe the condition of your world with the heart and mind of Jesus. Know the Gospels, read the Scriptures enough to measure your world's events against the horizon of the reign of God. Listen to the Scriptures and hear in them the cries of your world. Listen with the ear of your heart, with the ear of your anointed imagination; listen with the ear of personal and social conscience shaped by the Gospels. Reading the signs of the times through the lens of the Gospel is *prophetic* work. You are anointed as *prophet,* as Isaiah says and as Jesus quotes in the synagogue:

> The Spirit of the Lord is upon me,
>
> because he has anointed me
>
>> to bring glad tidings to the poor.
>
> He has sent me to proclaim liberty to
>
>> captives
>
> and recovery of sight to the blind,
>
>> to let the oppressed go free,
>
> and to proclaim a year acceptable to the
>
>> Lord.[89]

Our world today is all too full of people who are poor, who are captives traded in slavery, people who are crushed by oppression with no way to liberate themselves from their oppressors, with no means to escape famine, poverty, civil war, or genocide. These words of "glad tidings," impossible though they may sound, are the words that have been given to you. Act on them.

---

[88] I write these words as the Occupy Wall Street movement spreads across the nation. While the movement struggles for the words of a clear and compelling message, I have the unmistakable hunch that the Holy Spirit is at work in these raw attempts to read "the signs of the times" through a prophetic lens: "Wall Street prophets," so to speak, challenging Wall Street profits.

[89] Luke 4:18–19; see Isaiah 61:1–2. As noted earlier, in St. Luke's Gospel this prophetic passage marks the inauguration of Jesus' public ministry.

In Baptism and Confirmation you have been anointed, consecrated, set apart as Jesus was, to harness your heart's passion for God, to be a *prudent steward* of the life God has given you, to govern your relationships with purity of heart, humility, equity, and mercy. You have been anointed to this *kingly* work of *divine governance* of your life and of the concerns of your world. Jesus affirms this right governance in describing "the faithful and prudent servant, whom the master has put in charge of his household to distribute … food at the proper time" (Matthew 24:45). And in the great parable of the Judgment of the Nations, Jesus asserts that, when the king comes at the end of time, he will reward those who have lived as worthy stewards of God's own generosity, mercy, and inclusive love.[90] Much has been entrusted to you already, and over the course of your life much more will be entrusted to you—material goods, relationships, the needs and concerns of others, responsibilities of work. In Baptism and Confirmation you have been anointed to exercise right governance and good stewardship over these dimensions of your world.

The Vocational Connection

How can you discover the vocational dimension and actually live this unique and powerful anointing as priest, prophet, and king (or wise steward) in your daily life? I offer three practical steps.

First, *wake up to your world* and notice what it looks like. Notice where the grace is, and where the anguish.[91] Wake up your heart and mind to what is going on; notice what in the world is not right. Notice the distortions and brokenness and spiritual infections that we have mistakenly come to accept as

---

[90] See Matthew 25:34–40.

[91] Theologian Jon Sobrino describes this interior or existential waking up as "awakening from the sleep of inhumanity." An excellent examination of this notion of interior awakening is presented in John Neafsey's book, *A Sacred Voice is Calling: Personal Vocation and Social Conscience* (Maryknoll NY: Orbis, 2006); see especially chapter 9, "Social Conscience: Awakening from the Sleep of Inhumanity."

normal. It is so easy to become numbed to the daily news feed of devastation, injustice, and human anguish that we tune it out and think nothing more of it. Or we career in addictive fixation from one late-breaking news trauma to the next, real human anguish packaged to satisfy our unquenchable thirst for shock and drama. Our collective threshold for violence and violation rises increasingly higher, rendering us less and less able to "do anything about it." The forces of evil in our world triumph when we—especially we who are anointed in the Holy Spirit—feel numb to human anguish and incapable of taking action against injustice and the scourge of hopelessness.

Awaken your imagination to *God's* view of things and God's willing. In your daily prayer, and as you take in the daily news, ask God: "What breaks *your* heart today? What gives *you* hope?" And then wait attentively for the unexpected answers, delivered in unexpected moments. Awaken your conscience to guide you to right action, in the ways that you are able, to protect life in all of its dimensions from violence and to bring about God's equity, mercy, justice, and peace. Expand your capacity for God in your world by the choices you make, by intentional actions which affect others in ways that are healing, encouraging, and life-giving. Through prayer intentionally create capacity for the Holy Spirit to be the active agent in your life, sanctifying and animating your mind, your understanding, your conscience, and your imagination.

Will this be easy? Will it be convenient? Probably not. But it will move you from the close-in world of your immediate concerns to the expansive world of God's concerns.

Second, *take action.* Apply yourself. Because you already are anointed you do not have to waste time trying to figure out what action to take. The Holy Spirit already is at work, prompting your imagination, nudging open your mind and your heart, and removing the obstacles that stand in the way. All you have to do is ask, and then be open to the answers. God has absolutely no interest in all the reasons why we think we cannot act with the power of the Holy Spirit and in the place of the living Christ. God is passionate right now about healing, redeeming, restoring all of humankind and all of creation. And God is passionate about calling every ounce of your being—heart, soul, mind, and strength—into play for the good of this world which God still so loves. Stand up and receive the grace courageously, and then act on it.

Third, after you take action, *reflect on your experience.* Reflect back on the nature of the situation which called for your action and the moments when you were actually engaged in responding; notice what that experience was like for you. Did you feel fully present? energized? wholehearted? Did you feel as though the Holy Spirit was working through you? What was that like? Give words to your experience. Explore this experience, examine it, savor it, own it for the grace which it is. Fruitfulness in your actions may be a sign that you and the Holy Spirit are partnering in vocationally important ways, that God's calling for your life might be finding its particular direction, or might be coming into clearer focus, unfolding as you mature in your life into "the full stature of Christ."[92]

Equally important is your reflection on any discouraging results. When you were engaged in what you believed God was asking of you, did you feel out of your element? stressed? wanting to help but feeling inadequate? Did the crush of sacrifice overtake any sense of real engagement, or derail your intention to give yourself to God's willing and desiring? These responses might be important clues that God desires to redirect your passion and engage your commitment in some other way. You may find yourself needing to shift gears or reset your sights elsewhere on the horizon. Keep your heart and your mind open and available to God's prompting. The Holy Spirit is restless to get on with the work of redemption, the work of revealing the reign of God, and you remain uniquely anointed to stand in the place of Jesus, vested with the same authority by which

---

[92] See Ephesians 4:13.

he revealed the reign of God.

If all of this sounds "vocational"—it is. Your life has *your* name on it, a name spoken by God and etched upon the heart of God long before you saw the light of day. By God's design you have been anointed for a purpose—to be a unique expression today of the living Christ in the world you inhabit.

And if all of this sounds a little overwhelming as well, take heart. You do not stand alone. We will look next at what the Christian community owes each of its members as they mature toward their full stature in Christ.

Questions for Conversation

1. What two or three points can I glean from this chapter?

2. In what situations, or in what dimensions of my life, do I intentionally allow the Holy Spirit to lead me? Is it in workplace situations? family relationships? studies? civic engagement? volunteer activities? (Describe one or two situations in specific detail where you have experienced the Holy Spirit at work.)

3. What were the results? (Be specific.) What outcomes can I point to? Is there a pattern here of positive outcomes? of frustrated or inconsistent outcomes? (Describe as fully as possible.)

4. In what situations recently have I allowed my heart to get mixed up, as Jesus did, with the world's anguish? (Name them.) What consistent patterns do I find? What consistent "theme" of concerns seems to engage me? And what am I doing about it? (Be specific.)

4

NONE OF US STANDS ALONE

What the Christian Community Owes You

[L]ive in a manner worthy of the call you have received. … [Y]ou were also called to the one hope of your call; one Lord, one faith, one baptism …

Ephesians 4:1, 4–5

The word *confirmation* is surprisingly close, both in spelling and in sound, to another word with an equally important spiritual meaning: the word *conformation*. What connects these two words? The root of the word con*firm*ation means to make firm, to strengthen, to establish, to encourage or approve, to make authentic. All of these descriptors certainly apply to the spiritual strength and grace made available to us in the sacrament of Confirmation: to make firm *in Christ;* to strengthen *in Christ;* to establish, encourage, and approve *in Christ;* to receive the anointing of your authentic personhood and life *in Christ.*

Transformed for a Purpose

We can also think of Confirmation as the sacrament of "conformation," of being "conformed to Christ," a connective spiritual thread that weaves throughout the New Testament, especially in the letters of St. Paul. The root of the word con*form*ation means to make similar; to bring into harmony or agreement; to be shaped and formed in the image of another. Here St. Paul writes: "For those [whom God] foreknew he also predestined to be conformed to the image of his Son" (Romans 8:29).

Given that you are incapable of shaping your life completely independent from the forces and influences that surround you, how do you become conformed specifically to the image of Christ Jesus—especially as you live in the midst of so many countervailing forces? In clear and strong language St. Paul urges: "Do not conform yourself to this age but be transformed by the renewal of your mind, that you may discern what is the will of God" (Romans 12:2). This word *transformation,* too, carries important spiritual weight. To be transformed, in this context, means to be reshaped, reconfigured—not only the outer self but more importantly, the inner self, reshaped in attitude and intention in a way that enables you to undergo your deeper vocational work—becoming inseparably a part of Christ himself. St. Paul's words offer no small admonition, and they challenge us with no small task. And the challenge is this: How *can* you effectively resist being "conformed to this age"?

First of all, we need to be clear in our language and in our thinking. Does everything "in this age" need to be resisted? Let's take a closer look: Is "this age" a code phrase for the forces of evil? Or might it refer to the broad palette of all that is here now? The Gospel of St. John might argue for the former; the Synoptic writers—St. Matthew, St. Mark, and St. Luke—might argue for the latter. Since the earliest days of the church we have understood that we are "in this world but not of it"[93] Our identity lies elsewhere. The challenge of being church in our twenty-first century world is not so much the challenge of finding ways to hermetically seal ourselves against our culture as the challenge to be leaven in it,[94] to be salt, and light,[95] as Jesus was, and to dispel the darkness, as Jesus did.[96]

The challenge here—to be in the world but not of it—is huge, and vocational to the core, perhaps the greatest vocational challenge we can undergo. It is the challenge of giving flesh and spirit to God's foolish and relentless pursuit. We are challenged to say to the world what God might say and what Jesus often demonstrated: "We seek you out to engage you where you are, in God's work of redemption." This "foolish pursuit" describes the stance of the good shepherd[97] seeking that one lost sheep who probably already was high maintenance, nonconformist, intent on its own agenda, and quarrelsome to boot. You can survive being in the world but not of it only to the degree that your interior self and outer actions have been conformed to Christ.

No matter your age when you encounter the sacrament, in Confirmation you pass from being a spiritual child to becoming a spiritual adult. You cross a spiritual threshold where your anointing in the Holy Spirit empowers you to take your relationship with Jesus more intentionally, and to recognize that life in Christ, lived generously in the company of the Holy Trinity, is God's intent *for you* and for the full trajectory of your life. St. Paul feels so passionately about

---

[93] In his prayer on the night before his arrest, in St. John's Gospel, Jesus makes clear this point: "[Father,] I do not pray for the world but for the ones you have given me. ... [T]he world hated them, because they do not belong to the world any more than I belong to the world. I do not ask that you take them out of the world but that you keep them from the evil one" (see John 17:6–15).

[94] See Matthew 13:33 and Luke 13:21, where Jesus compares the reign of God to the beneficial effect of leaven worked into a mass of dough.

[95] Regarding salt, see Matthew 5:13; Mark 9:50; Luke 14:34–35; regarding light see Matthew 5:14–16; Mark 4:21–22; Luke 8:16–17, 11:33. In St. John's Gospel Jesus refers to himself as the light of the world (see John 8:12, 9:5, and 12:46).

[96] See St. John's description of the Word: "the light [that] shines in the darkness, / and the darkness has not overcome it" (John 1:5). See also John 8:12, where Jesus refers to himself as "the light of the world."

[97] See John 10:11.

being conformed to Christ, and having the mind of Christ, that he writes: "[I wish] to know [Christ] and the power of his resurrection and [the] sharing of his sufferings by being conformed to his death, if somehow I may attain the resurrection from the dead" (Philippians 3:10–11). These words of St. Paul are meant to be our own words as well, because the divine passion that impels St. Paul to write them is the passion of the same Holy Spirit who dwells within each one of us.

In Confirmation you enter a stage in your maturing spiritual life in which you now take on more *personal* responsibility for Jesus' mission in your world. The partnership is sealed, *confirmed,* and set in motion. Spiritually you move from being a follower of Jesus (a disciple) to being one who is anointed in his Spirit, equipped for real spiritual work, and sent for a purpose (an apostle).

Confirmed, Conformed, and Not Alone

Indeed, St. Paul ultimately was conformed to Christ in his martyrdom. Tradition tells us that Paul suffered death by beheading. Chances are good that your life will not follow the same path as his. But as you conform your heart, your mind, your understanding and attitude, and your willing freely to God's perfect willing, you begin to stand more intentionally, more readily, and more effectively in the place of the living Christ for the good and the salvation of others.

This "being conformed to Christ" can sound like lonely work, like Jacob wrestling with the angel in the course of the night.[98] Indeed, each of us must wrestle alone with larger unseen forces. The good news here is that while you must wrestle alone, in your commitment of faith you do not need to stand alone. The first letter of St. Peter offers encouragement here: "Be sober and vigilant. Your opponent the devil is prowling around like a roaring lion looking

---

[98] See Genesis 33:23–33.

for [someone] to devour. Resist him, steadfast in faith, *knowing that your fellow believers throughout the world undergo the same sufferings"* (1 Peter 5:8–9, emphasis added). In fact, you cannot stand alone in the tremendous work of giving witness to your authentic life-in-God, nor should you have to, as you mature toward the full authority of your anointing. Sometimes the ones who think they have to "go it alone" forget, or perhaps have never understood, that they are part of a larger Christian community, a vast network of holy ones who all wrestle toward their full stature in Christ, and who are there to support one another in growing toward spiritual adulthood.

At the same time, the Christian community itself wrestles its way toward awakening to its collective anointing and dynamic participation in the Lord's mission of revealing the reign of God. Sometimes the ones who feel consigned to stand alone have never heard from others within the Christian community that their active participation in the life of the church actually matters—not only to the church but equally to the world.

When you were baptized, you were baptized into the body of Christ. When you are spiritually nourished in Eucharist, you approach the table of the Lord in communion with others, as part of the community of the Beloved, engaging in intimate table fellowship with the risen Lord Jesus. In the closing rite of the Mass the entire assembly is commissioned once again to return to its vast and varied mission field beyond the borders of the church parking lot.

Roots of Rebellion

That mission field is the world as we encounter it and come to know it, the world as it engages our heart, our mind, and our Christian imagination. In a beautiful passage in the Book of Isaiah the prophet declares:

The Lord GOD has given me

  a well-trained tongue,

That I might know how to speak to the

    weary

  a word that will rouse them.

Morning after morning

  he opens my ear that I may hear;

And I have not rebelled,

  have not turned back. (Isaiah 50:4–5)

"I have not rebelled," the prophet says. Rebellion—pulling away from one's roots in a less than graceful way—has long defined the culture of North American youth, and has become the engine of a highly profitable market segment of the American economy. Youth began rebelling in droves as marketing moguls seized control of our culture's better senses. And "midlife crisis" has now become the market-driven catalyst to bust loose and invent "a new me." Rebellion is the opposite of obedience which, as the prophet Isaiah suggests, means "to open the ear," or *to listen with the ear of the heart.* "Morning after morning," the prophet seems to say, "though I could have rebelled, the Lord God renders me obedient." The young King Solomon may have had feelings of rebellion, too, but had the good sense to submit himself to the Lord God for wisdom on how to govern the Israelites. "Give your servant, therefore," he prayed, "an understanding heart" (1 Kings 3:9), or, "a listening heart." *Teach me,* he seems to say, *how to lean into you and trust.*

Quite contrary to this "leaning into God," today's sports and entertainment, personal electronics, clothing and gear, and advertising industries make a killing off of young people's urge to rebel, to stand apart and carve their separate identity. "Image is everything," young people are urged to believe as they separate from home and from all that has sheltered and formed them, and set out in search of their own identity. And the lure of personal rebellion is not confined to the younger generation. Rebellion can sometimes be the response of choice for men and women at any age when the hard work of "being conformed," especially by commitments of great personal cost, threatens their notion of self-identity or personal freedom.

Yet for every baptized Christian, image *is* everything. Genesis proclaims that every one of us was made in the image and likeness of God, and God pronounced every one of us "very good!"[99] St. Paul reminds us that Christ himself is "the image of the invisible God, / the firstborn of all creation" (Colossians 1:15). Every one of us is a part of "all creation." Our image, our unique expression of God's unfathomable goodness, matters immensely in this world. Rebellion, here, and the rejection of this divine image, often expresses resistance to the hard work of growing beyond the cult of the self in order to engage in mature and morally responsible ways in the larger world.

Beyond Rebellion: Missional Separation

But this whole business of rebellion, or resistance, or rejection, is of a very different nature from the necessary *vocational* separation from family and one's familiar milieu in order to discover and claim and embrace one's unique identity in Christ. This vocational stepping away is what I call "missional separation," which even Jesus underwent in his youth. The word *missional*, surprisingly, does not appear in my dictionary, so I will explain to you what I mean. "Missional," based on the word *mission*, comes from the Latin root *missio*, which means "to be sent" in order to accomplish an important work.

---

[99] See Genesis 1. Seven times in this chapter the message is expressed: "God saw how good" it was.

Jesus sent his apostles "on a mission" to reveal the reign of God.[100]

So missional separation refers to the difficult, maturing work (and sometimes the real heartache) of separating from family, friends, and your familiar world in order to follow Jesus in a particular, more mature, and personally committed way. We may think that missional separation is an interior work unique to the young adult stage. But people in later stages of life often awaken to a deeper calling, or awaken to the fact that they have entered a new personal era, such as the "empty nest" stage, or retirement, or widowhood, which opens up to them the possibility of new ways of living their faith. For some, missional separation may mean stepping away from decades of work which no longer holds meaning or which lacks a compelling sense of fruitfulness and fulfillment. For others, later on, missional separation may mean detaching from adult children and grandchildren in order to engage in those dimensions of life which require a maturing of purpose in a more existential— and sometimes lonely—way. In the later stages of life, missional separation may mean loss of lifelong capacities and entry into the solitary work of decreasing so that the Lord himself might increase and perfect his work within the soul.

Navigating well through the missional separations of early life becomes a worthy apprenticeship for the many separations you will know in the course of your vocational journey.

No matter your stage in life, Jesus speaks with a decisive edge of the challenge of missional separation, with words that cut clean across all generations: "Whoever loves father or mother more than me is not worthy of me, and whoever loves son or daughter more than me is not worthy of me" (Matthew 10:37). These are painful and sobering words, and may evoke pushback, or may make us uncomfortable in our attachments. It is one thing for me to say, "Lord, I am not worthy of you." But here the Lord himself tells me

---

[100] See Jesus' sending out of the Twelve (Matthew 10; the entire chapter goes into detail on what this missioning will entail for them); see also Jesus' sending out of the seventy–two (Luke 10:1–12).

outright that I am not worthy of him if I cling even to my familiar relationships in a way that would hold me back from following him wholeheartedly. These are stinging words indeed.

Undergoing missional separation does not mean that God's willing for your life has become, or soon will become, perfectly clear. It seldom is. Undergoing missional separation means that you are willing, oftentimes at some personal cost, to step apart from the familiar in order to create capacity for God's willing to be revealed in time and circumstance in your particular life. Missional separation requires a generous and loving spirit of faithfulness and obedience because God's plan is *not* perfectly clear, and you discover that you are willing to act on a hunch, an intuition, or an unexpected opening of possibility.

We get an early glimpse of Jesus' missional separation in the Gospel of St. Luke. Mary and Joseph retraced their steps back to Jerusalem when they discovered that the twelve-year-old Jesus was missing among their clan. After three days of anxious searching they found the youth in the temple, sitting among the teachers, listening and asking them questions. St. Luke tells us: "[H]e said to them, 'Why were you looking for me? Did you not know that I must be in my Father's house?'" (Luke 2:49). His parents must have felt stunned, rebuffed, confused. Parents today can feel that same way, especially when a son or daughter chooses a path in life that does not hold the promise of fulfilling their well-intentioned dreams.

Why were you looking for me? These are not the words of a twelve-year-old in rebellion; rather, here we find an example of missional separation, the moving away from family and the familiar in order to enter onto the very personal path which God has mapped out. Whether it feels this way or not, receiving your unique anointing for *your* particular life in Christ is always full of grace. Still, if you are young, or at a critical threshold in your life—especially if you have experienced a wounding of spirit—you can easily feel pressured to reject what has been familiar and predictable and sustaining for you. If you awaken to this work of missional separation in mid or later life, you may feel at first the urge to rail against all that has sustained you and reject the relationships, family bonds, your work environment, or even your entire career or profession as suddenly intolerable. But let grace prevail in this process of separation. Something is starting to shift. Relationships, predictable patterns, even your limited notion and images of God, may begin to fall apart.

This is not so much "bad" or "good" as it is *invitational*—your personal invitation to encounter God in a new and spiritually more mature way. It is a time to courageously enter into God-as-Mystery, a time to recenter in this God beyond your understanding, to recenter in Jesus the living Christ and in the Holy Spirit, and to stay faithful in prayer, listening intently with the ear of the heart. This work of missional separation is a necessary first step in discerning God's vocational intentions for your life. *Let grace prevail.*

What You Deserve

As you mature spiritually you will find increasingly that you cannot stand alone in living your Christian witness. None of us can, nor should you have to. This wisdom is not always perfectly obvious to young people, nor to people of any age who find themselves more at the margins than at the center of parish life. Needing the strength of the Christian community is not necessarily the same—and certainly not of the same spirit—as simply "getting to Mass every Sunday."[101] Oftentimes it takes the birth of that first child, or some other life-changing event, sometimes traumatic, to awaken us to the real and vital need to immerse ourselves among others who share a vibrant Christian faith.

---

[101] While for good reason the church takes most seriously the obligation of Sunday Mass (see *CCC* 1389), my focus here is on the vital need to draw life and meaning and interior strength from the body of Christ in its local expression. See my article, "Obliged by Love: Rediscovering the Real Obligation of Sunday Mass," *Today's Catholic Teacher* (April–May 2011), 84–85.

There will come times when you will need—and *deserve*—the living faith of others when your own faith seems thin, shattered, confused, or merely adrift. And times will come when you will need—and *deserve*—to participate intentionally and wholeheartedly in the gathering of God's anointed ones around the table of Word and Eucharist, celebrating the sacred mysteries and being fed, spiritually fed, on the Bread of Life. Over the course of your life you will undergo many situations where you will need—and *deserve*—the steadfast witness of faith of all of the members of the Christian community, perhaps more than you can imagine now.[102]

And equally important, the Christian community needs and deserves *your* expressions of living faith—now and through all the stages of your life. No matter your age or state in life, you are a vital part of the greater church of the twenty-first century. It is not a stretch to say that in your local church, within your parish, there is a particular pew, or a particular chair, which has *your* name on it. No one else can fill your space. No one else can "stand in" for you. No one else can receive or carry out your particular commissioning. No one else can live your life or give lifelong expression to your unique anointing in Christ. That mission is fully yours.[103]

Your Faith Community, a Dynamic Relationship

A parish is far more than the gathering of people who come for worship on Sunday morning and who then, for the most part, go off in their separate directions for the rest of the week. Over time the threads of genuine caring and friendship—celebration in joyful times and support in times of loss and grieving,

---

[102] I recall the prolonged illness my father underwent. The packed-to-capacity church at his funeral Mass offered immeasurable spiritual sustenance and consolation to my mother and our family at this most painful time in our lives.

[103] I wrote similar words in a note to a young man who stopped attending Mass shortly after he was confirmed. The following Sunday he was in attendance and came up to me afterward and thanked me for the note. "I didn't realize that my being here would matter to anyone," he said. "It matters to me," I replied.

bonds formed and strengthened by sacramental life—weave together a vibrant Christian community. Many parishes today are an unlikely mix of people of various backgrounds and generations, people who normally would have no reason to touch each other's life, much less stand together to pray and sing, if it were not for the risen Lord Jesus and the sacramental life of the church drawing them together again and again. And because the risen Lord and this sacramental life do draw them together, people within the community of faith know that they are in it together "for the long haul," for the long vocational journey into Christ. Infused by the Holy Spirit, the Christian community itself awakens over time to its particular mission, its own unique vocation. Or sometimes that mission and vocation are planted as a seed, compelling enough at the start to call forth a parish community into being. Part of that mission and vocation of the Christian community is to carry each one of us from spiritual childhood across the threshold to spiritual adulthood.[104] And that mission is not accomplished all at once.

What does the Christian community owe you—no matter your age or state in life, or the number of years you have been a member of the parish? These three things are essential:

First, your faith community owes you *ongoing personal acknowledgement* and genuine welcome as the spiritually emerging person that you are. If you are young, or if you are new to the parish, if you have been away for a decade or two, or even if you have been a longtime member but find yourself more at the margins than at the center, you still have a rightful place within this body of believers. Sometimes people at the margins may have to take the initiative to enable others to acknowledge their presence and draw them gently into the community of the Beloved. You deserve to be acknowledged as a vital member of the body of Christ.

---

[104] The four-workshop process of Awakening Vocations addresses and develops precisely this work of spiritual, missional, and vocational awakening of the parish community. A fuller description of this process can be found at http://www.awakeningvocations.com/awakeningvocations.html.

Second, your faith community owes you *resources* to help you to grow in every stage of life and in every dimension of your unique vocational journey.[105] These resources might include adult and young adult catechesis, guidance through major life transitions, immersion in Catholic social teaching, justice-based activism, mentoring, vocational guidance, even academic and professional coaching when that is needed and available.[106] It is important to ask for what you need. Seek it out. Be persistent. What you need for your spiritual and vocational growth may be what others also need, but did not know how to ask.

Third, your faith community owes you *challenge and encouragement*— through every state and stage in life. Specifically, your faith community owes you the challenge and encouragement to identify and use your gifts and talents, your time, your resources, and your imagination, appropriate to your life circumstances, for wholehearted engagement in revealing the reign of God. And when you have stepped forward to use your gifts and talents, your faith community owes you the means to reflect upon those experiences with deeper understanding, whether through one-to-one mentoring, homiletic insights into Gospel living, or formation in the skills of theological reflection on your life experiences.[107]

But the faith community, like every life-giving intentional community, requires a mutual engagement and the interaction of dynamic relationship, which means that in return for what you receive, you likewise owe some things

---

[105] A drawback of child-centered or even multigeneration family-centered parish catechesis is its inability to address the unique concerns and challenges of mature faith in adults whose faith development lies outside the family-focused curriculum.

[106] The "Core Team Immersion" portion of the Awakening Vocations process spells out resources appropriate to each constituent group within the parish. See http://www.awakeningvocations.com/awakeningvocations.html.

[107] A helpful resource on the techniques of theological reflection is Patricia O'Connell Killen and John de Beer's book, *The Art of Theological Reflection* (New York: Crossroad, 2002). For a narrative example of theological reflection, see my essay "Let Me See Your Face," in *Touching the Reign of God*. I discuss practical application of theological reflection in daily life in *Moving in God's Direction: Essentials of Christ-centered Spiritual and Vocational Direction* (Eugene, OR: Awakening Vocations, 2012).

to your parish community. And what might these be?

First, you owe your parish community *your faithful presence:* being present regularly and wholeheartedly—in worship, in ongoing spiritual and vocational formation, and in apostolic action.

Second, you owe your parish community *your ongoing engagement* in the missional life of the community itself. None of us is a Lone Ranger apostle; rather, we have been anointed into the body of Christ for active participation at *this* time, with *this* faith community, in the work of being light and salt and leaven for the world around us.

Third, you owe your parish community *your wholehearted Yes to God,* whether anyone is aware of the particular circumstances or the price of that Yes or not. You owe the Christian community the integrity of your faithfulness to God. There are no shortcuts in living out your steadfast commitment, and no situations where your spiritual and moral integrity does not matter. None of us has the privilege of some private moral understanding "between Jesus and me." Our lives are inextricably woven together into the one body of the living Christ. Each of us is anointed for a worthy purpose, both within the faith community and in every dimension of our private and public life.

Yes, Confirmation may seem like a one-time event. But as you can see, it unfolds, reveals itself, and comes to fullness over the course of a lifetime. Confirmation is God's way of saying: "I take your life seriously." And intellectually you might respond, "I get it." But I am convinced that it takes a lifetime to let the mystery of God's confidence in you really sink in, all the way down to your bones and to the marrow of your bones.

Whether you are in your twenties, your forties, your sixties, or beyond, as you take the anointing of Confirmation more seriously, you grow into your more mature place within the Christian community. You are personally and uniquely called by God in Baptism and anointed in the Holy Spirit in

Confirmation. What comes next is actually *living* the anointed life. In Part II we will explore what this means.

Questions for Conversation

1. What two or three points can I glean from this chapter?

2. In stepping away from family or from a life that has been familiar to me, in order to respond to God's deeper calling, have I acted with rebellion? with grace? or with both? How so? What examples come to mind?

3. In what family, work, or other situations do I feel more likely to rebel or pull away? Is there a deeper vocational shift and spiritual awakening going on in me which I have disregarded or dismissed as merely a need to break away? or (if older) casually described as a "midlife crisis"? What does that crisis-rebellion-vocational awakening really look like for me? (Be specific.)

4. Where might I be now on the scale between rebellion and missional separation from the life I have known? If I have been rebelling, what relationships have been wounded in the process that need to be healed? With whom have I been obnoxious or even hurtful? (Be specific.) If I am experiencing missional separation in order to pursue a deeper calling in my life, how would I describe that experience?

PART II

LIVING THE ANOINTED LIFE

With this deeper understanding of Confirmation as a lifelong anointing in the Holy Spirit, we can now explore what this anointed life in Christ might look like. Even more important, we can now begin to identify ways to actively and competently discern God's willing in this sacramentally anointed life—your life—which God has given to you.

Part II, Living the Anointed Life, examines the effects of God's calling in the ways we live our lives. In the following chapters we will bring the relevance of Confirmation to the two main areas of human concern for every baptized man and woman: first, vocational lifestyle, and second, the actual living of God's calling. We will distinguish between "making decisions" and actually *discerning* God's willing.

Finally, we will look at a necessary and much needed fruit of sacramental anointing for today's world: Peacemaking as a core element and defining activity in Christian life.

SINGLE, MARRIED, CELIBATE

A Deeper Discernment of Vocational Lifestyle

As a body is one though it has many parts, and all the parts of the
body, though many, are one body, so also Christ. … Now you are
Christ's body, and individually parts of it.

1 Corinthians 12:12, 27

I listened recently to a talk on vocations, and found myself sitting on
the edge of my chair with the speaker's opening statement. Not because this
opening statement presented a helpful perspective on the nature of God's
calling, but because it didn't. "There are two vocational lifestyles," our speaker
said, "priesthood and marriage." The sentence, so simple and direct,
immediately emblazoned itself in my memory. This unhelpful teaching was
reiterated, word for word, toward the close of the talk. Unhelpful yes, but why?

Any meaningful or helpful conversation around "vocational lifestyle" must be situated in the broader context of the nature of God's calling and our free and loving response. And the starting point for conversation is distinguishing between *who* God calls you to *be* and *what* God calls you to *do.*

Before you are sacramentally—and therefore vocationally—anointed to "do something," you are anointed to "be someone"—specifically, the person whom God has desired from all eternity to stand uniquely in the place of the living Christ in this place and time. One essential way you mature into this person of God's desiring is through your vocational lifestyle—the way you live your life, as single, married, or celibate. Discernment of vocational lifestyle seldom comes quickly or easily. Nor can discernment of vocational lifestyle ride on any assumptions nor be shaped or pressured by expectations—whether your own or the expectations of others.

Discernment of vocational lifestyle is a discernment concerning *modes of relationship* with others, as uniquely expressed through single, married, or celibate life.[108] The angst among many teenagers and young adults in our broader culture today, over not only "sexual orientation" but "gender identity," indicates just how strong run the currents of confusion over the focus of authentic personhood, both individually and in modes of relationship with others.

For those who are anointed into Christian life, the starting point for discerning vocational lifestyle is not "me" but *God's desiring* of me in one form of relationship or another—as single, married, or celibate. Each of these lifestyles is oriented toward fruitfulness in the reign of God, but fruitfulness only for those who are authentically called by God to that particular lifestyle.[109]

---

[108] The important distinctions between single and celibate life will be discussed later in this chapter.

[109] For portions of the material presented here I am indebted to Nemeck and Coombs for their groundwork on vocational lifestyles in *Discerning Vocations.*

Three Vocational Lifestyles, One Calling

What is Christian vocational lifestyle? In simplest terms, it means the way you live the "relationship" part of the life that God has in mind for you. And given that God, in the three persons of the Holy Trinity, is all about relationship, we must closely examine just how we come to an understanding of *who* we are in relationship with God, and therefore *how* we are in relationship with self and others. Apart from the work you do, your Christian vocational lifestyle is the way you grow and mature over the course of your lifetime, through one mode of relationship or another, into the fullness of your authentic personhood. The vocational lifestyle to which God calls you serves as the platform from which you engage in your particular work of revealing the reign of God over the course of your life.

These three vocational lifestyles also shape the way you are in relationship with another (in marriage) or with others (in singlehood or in celibate life). Each of these vocational lifestyles expresses a specific and ever maturing self-identity in God. Each vocational lifestyle also shapes how you perceive and experience your life, and the freedom with which you engage in your world as one of God's anointed. And each of these lifestyles points to the same truth: *I become fully alive in God by freely embracing the particular way God calls me into relationship.* Each vocational lifestyle is "best" only for those who are genuinely called by God to that particular way of life. Let's examine each of these lifestyles to see what all of this means.

A Closer Look at Christian Singlehood

In Christian vocational language, *single* is often confused with *celibate*. Oftentimes the terms are unhelpfully used interchangeably. But the two are distinct from each other in a vocationally crucial way. *Single* means, quite simply, not married but *open to the possibility of marriage.* That last phrase is the distinctive part of the definition of singlehood. As a vocational lifestyle, singlehood most often is transitional, leading either to marriage or to a celibate way of life. Every one of us starts out single. As we become more socially interactive in the teen and young adult years we become conscious—sometimes painfully self-conscious—of our singleness.

In our culture today "singleness" for anyone over the age of, say, twenty-five oftentimes equals social "incompleteness," as though you are not quite right unless you are part of "a couple." Socially, our culture seems determined to pair people up. No matter your age—whether you are in your early twenties and single or in your forties and recently divorced—you can oftentimes feel an unspoken pressure to "find someone" in order to feel like you socially fit in.[110] As a result, many unmarried people—and not only young adults—feel the social pressure to date, to show up at family gatherings or social events at least "not alone." Oftentimes family and friends can apply the most pressure, or "encouragement," for the single person to get married, or at least be connected to someone.[111] Sometimes the need to escape the taboo of social isolation leads people, and not only young adults, to "hook up" with whoever is available, with little interest in getting entangled in the demands of relational intimacy or its consequences.

For increasing numbers of single men and women of Christian faith, a current way out of the anguish of singlehood is faith-oriented matchmaking Web sites.[112] Perhaps you know first-hand, or have known, the pressures of

---

[110] Some of this pressure also has to do with the unease, or "shadow of loneliness," that couples can feel as they encounter in a single person, especially one who is widowed or divorced, the prospect of their own unwilled return to the single state, through widowhood or through divorce.

[111] An encouraging resource to help single men and women to become free of the exclusionary world of a "couples" culture and to experience a sense of community, inclusion, and wholeness in single life is Debra Farrington's little book, *One Like Jesus: Conversations on the Single Life* (Chicago: Loyola Press, 1999).

[112] My conversations with Catholic single men and women who have used such Web sites reveal that resort to these Web sites easily short-circuits a proper discernment of vocational lifestyle and sidesteps the deeper work of embracing God's willing. Finding "the right match" can easily become an answer to the prayer: "My will be done." Such self-directed management of vocational lifestyle, bereft of the scrutiny, patience, and joy of a deeper discernment, overlooks the key question: *Is God*

singlehood in navigating your way personally and socially through the young adult years. Keeping Jesus at the center of your relationships may sound simplistic, but cherishing and cultivating a living relationship with the risen Lord is absolutely essential to calm the confusion, to bring dignity, meaning, focus, and joy to your relationships, and to relieve the pressure to conform yourself socially to others' expectations. As St. Paul points out, the real challenge is to "conform yourself to Christ"[113] and to the modes and expressions of relationship that God has in mind.

In the Christian context, being single and "open to the possibility of marriage" is not the same as "steady dating" or any other sort of premature exclusive one-to-one involvement that seeks to beat back the pain of social isolation. Relationship for the Christian single person is first of all relationship with God, with the living Christ, and flowing from that relationship comes relationship with others. This single-hearted focus brings us to the very essence of chastity—where relationship with God becomes the source of all other relationships. Expressing chastity in relationships is the opposite of snatching what is not yours. The challenge of chastity is this: If your relationship with another person does *not* flow from or find its meaning within your relationship with God, you have no right to flirt with it, engage in it, touch it, or take it.

Singlehood as a vocational lifestyle is usually transitional, and is the norm for emerging young adults. Some people will grow further into adulthood in the single state, and for one reason or another will not marry, although they may remain open to marriage and perceive themselves as datable. Extended singlehood is not the same as being called to a celibate vocational lifestyle (more about this below). Sometimes the nature of one's current commitments— perhaps a demanding academic schedule, long work hours or extensive travel, or

---

even calling me to Christian married life, and to married life with this particular person? This question is exceedingly important following divorce, and even more so in the wake of multiple divorces, or even multiple broken engagements.

[113] See Romans 8:29 ("conformed to the image of his Son"); see also 12:2 ("Do not conform yourself to this age but be transformed ... that you may discern what is the will of God").

caring for ill or aging family members—can precede and seem to delay a calling to Christian married life. But if God desires you to enter into Christian marriage, then in the perfection of God's timing and God's willing all the right pieces will come into play. Assuming our cooperation, in God's timing there is no such thing as a "delayed vocation." Extended singlehood requires you to trust in God's plan and to be wholeheartedly engaged in the current circumstances of your life—hopeful yet living in peace, with openness of mind, heart, and spirit to the way things are at the moment and to the intentions of God.

The Christian single person is vocationally open to the possibility of not just any type of marriage but, specifically, to the sacramental life of Christian marriage. What does this mean? Let's turn now to the vocational lifestyle of Christian marriage.

A Closer Look at Christian Married Life

Married, for the Christian man and woman, means living in a consecrated perpetual, exclusive, intimate relationship with the other, centered in Christ, for fruitfulness and holiness, and outwardly focused for the good of others.[114] Christian marriage is the preeminent sacramental expression of God's covenant love for the church, for the intimate community of family life, and for the family of all humankind. As Pope John Paul II asserted in his talks on the theology of the body, Christian marriage is the continual outpouring of self in love for the sake of the other, an expression of the selfless outpouring of love which is the very essence of the Holy Trinity.[115]

A great depth of emotional, psychological, and spiritual maturing must take place before a man and a woman can enter freely and wholeheartedly into

---

[114] For a full and enlightening discourse on the sacrament of Matrimony, see *CCC* 1601–1654.

[115] See Christopher West's very approachable and readable presentation of Pope John Paul's thoughts, *Theology of the Body for Beginners: A Basic Introduction to Pope John Paul II's Sexual Revolution* (West Chester PA: Ascension Press, 2004).

such a profound lifelong exclusive commitment to each other in Christ. For each, the relationship with Christ must be shaped, expressed, and sustained in a steadfast practice of Christian faith. And each must be capable of reaching beyond their own concerns to be a means of life and holiness for the other. That's a tall order, and something that must be taken to heart in discerning the vocational lifestyle of Christian marriage.[116]

How do you discern whether God is calling you, first of all to Christian married life, and secondly, to marry this particular person? Christian marriage is a lifelong commitment of sacramental covenant love made in great faith, a commitment which must be supported by indicators and convictions born of the Holy Spirit and shared by both parties. Here are some critical elements that need to be in place in order for the man and the woman each to undergo this double discernment of a calling to Christian married life and to marry this particular person:[117]

- The couple must be sufficiently mature emotionally, psychologically, and sexually.
- The relationship must express sufficient self-understanding, self-identity, and understanding of the other.
- The couple must have sufficient interdependence and mutual self-surrender.
- They must have compatible religious convictions and desire for spiritual growth.
- The relationship must indicate that the couple can live in Christ-centered peace which reaches outward to others.
- The couple must experience a love that moves them toward a lifelong conjugal covenant.

---

[116] This high threshold of spiritual maturity for entry into Christian marriage may account in part for the startling percentage of divorce in Catholic marriages. Though actual statistics may be elusive, the divorce rate within the Catholic church, at least in the United States, seems to hover somewhere near the divorce rate within the general population.

[117] Compiled from Nemeck and Coombs, *Discerning Vocations*, 98–99.

- They must each have a compelling sense that God is calling them to Christian married life.
- Ultimately, the couple must experience themselves as incapable of *not* entering into this vocational life together for the rest of their lives.[118]

When a Christian marriage comes to an end—through divorce and annulment or through death of the spouse, at some point a fresh discernment of vocational lifestyle becomes appropriate. Divorce, Jesus pointed out, was never intended as the norm,[119] so the failure of the marriage bond holds the seeds of insight into the true course of one's vocational journey. Perhaps both parties were called by God to Christian married life but not to marry each other. Or perhaps one or both parties were called not to Christian married life but to Christian celibate life.[120]

When a Christian marriage comes to an end through the death of one spouse, the surviving spouse may know intuitively that the work of that calling as a married person has been fulfilled, and may turn toward more spiritually intimate relationship with the risen Lord, allowing God to make free claim on the widowed person's time, energies, or resources. Or the widowed spouse may begin, in time, to discern God's calling again to Christian married life. No matter the intuitive hunch, an active discernment of vocational lifestyle is

---

[118] In my spiritual and vocational direction practice I encounter many individuals who are in a Christian marriage or who have undergone divorce—some multiple times—and who realize by hindsight that they never were called by God to Christian married life but to Christian celibate life. Lay celibate life, they discover, was not part of the discernment conversation in their preparations for marriage.

[119] See Matthew 5:31–32, where Jesus delivers a teaching on divorce in his inaugural sermon. See also Matthew 19:3–9, where the Pharisees test Jesus on the law of Moses concerning divorce (based on Deuteronomy 24:1–4).

[120] One woman in her late sixties told me that she felt quite certain that she was not called to Christian celibate life. "I've been married five times," she explained. I asked, "Which of those marriages worked?" After a long silence, she admitted, "None of them. In fact I live alone now, in my own house, and I have a freedom I have never felt before. I can pray openly and freely whenever I want, I volunteer at the church and at the rest home. I feel like I've finally gotten my own life and I can live in peace with God and everyone." I told her that she had pretty much described the charism of Celibacy. After a stunned pause she openly wept. "You just made sense of my entire life," she said. "No one has ever told me this before."

appropriate when the deeper work of grieving has been completed.

If singlehood defines one's vocational lifestyle before marriage, where does celibacy fit in? And how is it different from singlehood?

A Closer Look at Christian Celibate Life

Celibate life, for the Christian man or woman, means living unmarried and chaste in a way that renders one especially available to God's purposes—in the church or in the world.[121] Living a lay celibate life does not mean that you are "what's left over" after everyone else has gotten paired up in marriage, as though discerning vocational lifestyle were a game of musical chairs.[122] The celibate man or woman experiences a *spiritual* fruitfulness which is just as life-giving to them as the fruitfulness of family for those called by God to Christian married life. Joy in spiritual fruitfulness is a hallmark of authentic celibate life.

The church today is blessed with a surprising number of lay celibate men and women, who discern not a calling to priesthood or to monastic, cloistered, or apostolic religious life, but to a wholehearted Christ-centered

---

[121] See Matthew 19:11–12, where Jesus speaks to his disciples about those who "are incapable of marriage"—in other words, eunuchs either by birth or by castration, or "spiritual eunuchs" by a divine calling which renders them existentially incapable of entering into or even considering marriage. We find in the Acts of the Apostles (8:26–40) the account of the Ethiopian eunuch who was a court official in service to the queen of Ethiopia—in fact, "in charge of her entire treasury" (v. 27). Those who were incapable of marriage were often placed in sensitive government positions because they would not be tempted to divulge court secrets over "pillow talk," nor did they covet more than their means allowed in order to support a family or to advance their social standing. Faithfulness and loyalty to those they served was a distinguishing trait of eunuchs. A similar single–hearted faithfulness and loyalty to the Lord is the distinguishing trait of true celibates, "spiritual eunuchs" in the reign of God.

[122] Somewhere in my late thirties or forties it occurred to me that if I were to marry now, I would probably have to choose among men "on the rebound." Indeed, one single friend sighed, "All the good ones are taken." One unmarried person of middle age confided, "I feel like a third nostril on the face of the church." While this observation may evoke a humorous response, it suggests a sad commentary on vocational resources available to lay men and women who are not married.

engagement in their lay life and service in the church or in the world.[123] Given the diminished percentages in recent decades of priests and religious for whom celibacy is a requirement, we can wonder: Why so many lay celibates? What *in the world* is God up to?

Celibate lay men and women can be found in any of the more demanding professions, in the arts or other creative endeavors, in social service, humanitarian, or public service agencies. Many of these professions demand full dedication of time and attention, sometimes with little financial security. Some celibate lay men and women are involved in international diplomacy, advocacy, and peacemaking. Celibate men and women are found among those in frontline community outreach, social work, and human services, among those who tend to the sick and sit with the dying. Some celibate men and women are rendered available—sometimes through physical incapacity—for a life of unusually effective intercessory prayer. The focus here is on spiritual fruitfulness in ways that would be difficult if one had rightful commitments to spouse and family.[124]

The Christian celibate man or woman has a healthy regard for Christian married life, but just cannot picture that way of life as their own calling. As celibate men and women mature in this vocational lifestyle they increasingly understand that even dating would be an interruption of their time and their focus, especially the focus of their heart. More importantly, they eventually come to instinctively understand that even "flirting" with the possibility of dating would do a subtle but no less real violence to the fine-tuned interior disposition of soul and mind and heart in relation to the Lord. For them, Christ

---

[123] This topic is addressed in great depth in my audio series, *Christian Celibate Life: Discerning the Authentic Gift* (Eugene, OR: Awakening Vocations, 2010), available at http://www.awakening vocations.com/store.html.

[124] Dorothy Day writes in her autobiography *The Long Loneliness* of the young men just back from the First World War who came to the Catholic Worker, many with families they had to support. "[This] voluntary apostolate [the Catholic Worker] was for the unwilling celibate and for the unemployed, *as well as* for the men and women, *willing* celibates, who felt that running hospices, performing the works of mercy, working on farms, *was* their vocation, just as definitely a vocation as that of the professed religious." See Dorothy Day, *The Long Loneliness: The Autobiography of Dorothy Day* (San Francisco: Harper & Row, 1952, 1981), 187 (emphasis added).

truly is the center of their life, and relationship with him distinctively shapes and animates all of their other relationships, commitments, their overall way of being, and their engagement in the church and in the world.

Living the celibate lifestyle does not automatically mean that you are called to priesthood or consecrated religious life. Discernment of a calling to priesthood or religious life involves a different set of considerations *in addition to* discernment of a calling to authentic celibate life.[125] Christian celibate life is a positive and distinctive calling in its own right, and because it expresses so deeply the core of one's personhood it cannot effectively be "required" as a condition of ministry or mission. Either one has the gift, or charism, of celibacy, or one does not. A person cannot successfully reconfigure this core dimension of their personhood to meet other objectives, no matter how worthy or necessary these other objectives may be deemed. Celibacy is a source of spiritual fruitfulness, fulfillment, grace, and holiness for those who are genuinely called to this way of life. Living the celibate life without being gifted by God to do so can often lead to a persistent restlessness, spiritual frustration, and ultimately an interior crisis of personhood.[126]

Because the celibate vocational lifestyle renders one so open in a relationally solitary way to God's purposes, this unusual gift and calling must be clearly and convincingly discerned before a man or a woman can make a lifetime commitment to, say, celibate priesthood or consecrated celibate life within a religious community. As with the Christian married lifestyle, the Christian celibate lifestyle—*if you are called to it*—will open you to

---

[125] While married clergy can be found in the traditionally celibate Roman Catholic priesthood, they enter into active ministry as already married ordained clergy in one of the sacramental-liturgical denominations. A requirement of celibacy remains the norm for Roman Catholic clergy in the United States.

[126] Nemeck and Coombs address the concerns related to assuming a celibate lifestyle in order to qualify for ministry or membership in professed religious life when an actual calling to celibate life is not present. See their *Discerning Vocations,* 122–129. The *assumption* that one pursuing priesthood or professed religious life is called to, and gifted for, celibate life parallels the *assumption* that those pursuing Christian married life are called to, and gifted for, the vocational lifestyle of marriage. These assumptions are neither valid nor acceptable in the vocational discernment process.

extraordinary joy and fruitfulness, and become your sure path to holiness.

While both of these vocational lifestyles involve a "dying to self in service to the other," which is what the living of vows means, neither lifestyle is characterized by a diminishment of personhood in order to meet the demands of God's calling. In fact, each of these lifestyles, faithfully and lovingly lived, calls forth and affirms the dignity of one's personhood. Whatever the vocational lifestyle to which you are called, God's joy is meant to infuse and animate every dimension of your life, rendering your life fruitful in the reign of God.

Setting the Stage to Discern Vocational Lifestyle

Discerning—or discovering—your vocational lifestyle is not meant to be a source of interior anguish. Nor is discerning your vocational lifestyle a guessing game where God knows and you get to figure it out. Discerning your vocational lifestyle is a *process* that unfolds as you mature spiritually, emotionally, socially, and psychologically, and as you become responsibly engaged in your life, in your relationship with Jesus and his church, and in your relationships with others.

First, what does this word *discernment* mean? Discerning is not at all the same as "deciding." To discern means, in simplest terms, to cut away what does not belong so that you can see more clearly what God would have you see.[127] Discerning means looking for signs of God's willing amid the wide cluster of relationships, circumstances, commitments, inclinations, actions, attitudes, and possibilities that shape your life. Vocational discernment requires turning down the volume, getting rid of empty and distracting activities, and

---

[127] Legend has it that someone once asked the sculptor Michelangelo how he carved his masterpiece *David.* The craftsman replied, "I stood before the block of marble and removed from it all that was not David." Discerning, or discovering, one's authentic self vocationally involves something of that same "removing" of what does not belong in order to discover what does belong—or what is emerging.

materially and spiritually simplifying your life.[128] Deciding—a very different activity with a very different outcome—is about *you* making choices about what *you* think will best serve *your* interests. The difference between discerning and deciding is the difference between praying "Thy will be done" and "My will be done."

If you are young, most likely your vocation right now is to participate in and contribute to family life if you are living at home, and to engage wholeheartedly in your studies, your spiritual formation, your work, your relationships. It also is the time when you begin to notice your world, the world around you—your school, your workplace, your neighborhood, your town, and the circumstances of the greater world that engage your attention and call forth your response. Your vocation right now is also to develop a sense of your social self—yourself in relationship to others, and, equally important, your emerging social concern for, and active engagement in, your world.

If you are in young adulthood, you are at a time in your life when it is necessary to actively develop *personal* conscience for the moral choices you already are making and will be making as you mature, and the moral challenges you already are confronting and will be confronting in years to come. Developing a clear personal conscience now lays the foundation for patterns of clear moral choice making which animate your life in Christ. Early adulthood also is a time to actively develop *social* conscience formed by the whole of the Gospels and Jesus' teachings. Such formation attunes you to spiritual awareness of moral imbalances and injustices in your world, and equally attunes you to the ways in which God desires to touch the world through you for the cause of life, justice, mercy, and peace.[129]

---

[128] One downside of today's social media is its addictive preoccupation with much of life's superficialities. A helpful way to eliminate any sort of clutter is to ask: Will this matter twenty years from now? Will it matter twenty days from now—or even twenty minutes from now?

[129] A very thorough, well researched, and challenging resource on formation of social conscience is John Neafsey's book, *A Sacred Voice is Calling,* noted above.

It is not unusual to enter into your middle or even later years and discover a blind spot with regard to discernment of vocational lifestyle or the arduous work of awakening in a mature way to personal and social conscience. That is why it is so important to press for ongoing adult faith development as a vital dimension of parish life, as noted earlier. We should be at least as well equipped for real spiritual work according to our gifts and calling as we are for the work of our daily life. Mature Christ-centered spiritual work matters immensely in addressing the needs and challenges of our twenty-first century world.

At any point in your life you can begin the work of detecting patterns of grace and effectiveness and gathering clues about God's willing for your life, and gain a sense of where the Holy Spirit is bearing fruit. The best place to begin discerning your vocational lifestyle is where you are in your life right now. There is no need to project out into the future, as though God's intention for your life will be achieved, or at least clearly revealed, at some future milestone. Right here, right now, is the perfect and necessary starting point in the discovery of what God desires to accomplish in you and through you.

Five Encouragements for Discerning Vocational Lifestyle

How can you acquire a clear understanding of God's willing for your vocational lifestyle? No matter where you are in your life, these five encouragements can help you to make sense of God's subtle movement in relationships and life circumstances:

First, it is easier to get *a general sense of God's movement* in your life, especially in your relationships and the quality of intimacy and generosity of your interaction with others, than to discern God's calling in specific situations. If someone you've secretly had a crush on has finally noticed you, that does not necessarily mean that this person is "the one." It does not even mean that you are being called to Christian married life. Resist the urge to draw hasty conclusions based on "connecting the perfectly obvious dots." A kiss is not a commitment.

Second, sometimes it is easier to *see what God's willing is not* rather than to discern what God's willing *is*. Noticing and accepting a recurring pattern of "No" is a valuable part of the vocational lifestyle discernment process. If you keep pressing (or "praying hard") for, say, the perfect marriage partner, and still get the same empty results, accept this negative as a positive step in discerning (literally, cutting away) what does not fit in the picture of your life in order to more clearly discover what does.[130]

Third, always remember that *God does not set you up to fail.* We human beings are perfectly skilled at setting ourselves up for failure.[131] Rather, God is passionately interested—indeed, fully invested—in moving you toward faithfulness, trust, right action, and the experience of fruitfulness and joy that come with living in the Holy Spirit. The vocational lifestyle to which God calls you is perfectly suited to your being-in-God.

Fourth, *a regular, honest, and ever-deepening prayer life* is essential to discern your vocational lifestyle. Being regularly with God in prayer forms the very core of our most intimate and generous human relationships, and is the necessary starting point and the fulfillment of relationship with others. You simply cannot cut corners on prayer and come out with reliable results. Everything about your life, and every dimension of your life, *begins in* God, is set in motion *by* God, and ultimately is entirely *for* God. Which means that everything about your life is about your relationship—and the quality of your

---

[130] Sometimes people say: "I've been praying on this for years and so far God has not answered my prayer." Often God *has* answered the prayer, and the answer was *No*, or sometimes *Yes, but not according to your plan*. I frequently encounter married couples who find themselves unable to conceive and bring forth children, and who resort to medical intervention to achieve pregnancy. Such intervention is not without grave vocational and moral concern.

[131] David Whyte has an apt expression for this self-sabotage, observing that "we are the one part of creation that can refuse to be itself." See *Crossing the Unknown Sea,* 7.

relationship—with God. Give your life the regular prayerful attention and spiritual nourishment it needs and deserves.

Fifth, be *willing to experiment with possibilities.* If you perceive yourself as datable, seek social situations that give the Holy Spirit the opportunity to set a deeper work in motion. If you are married, engage as a couple in activities that give the Holy Spirit the opportunity to touch your world through the two of you in ways that can come about only by virtue of this particular marriage. If you feel drawn to celibate life, notice the moments when you feel most alive and most authentically yourself-in-God. Notice the circumstances and the recurring patterns of circumstances when you find yourself most at peace, engaged, effective, and spiritually fruitful.

When doors open that seem to lead to fulfillment of your vocational lifestyle, go through them with your heart and mind open to God's grace and guidance. They might be the right doors, or they may be doors that ultimately will lead you to where you need to go by a path you could not have imagined. Pay attention to the unexpected nudges, inspirations, and unbidden graces of the Holy Spirit. Give thanks daily for this guidance, and give such guidance the space it needs to happen. Reflect on God's guidance. Cherish it.

An honest and careful discernment of vocational lifestyle lays the foundation for discerning the vocational work for which you have been anointed. Right "being" enables right "doing." Next we will explore the difference between career and calling, and consider some helpful steps to discern what God is up to in your life.

Questions for Conversation

1. What two or three points can I glean from this chapter?

2. Where am I in the process of discerning my vocational lifestyle? Has anything changed—or possibly remained "stuck" and unfruitful—that prompts a fresh discernment of my vocational lifestyle? What relationships do I need to let go? What relationships do I need to repent? What relationships do I need to cherish more, or take more seriously? (Be specific.)

3. If I am single, can I easily imagine myself in a generous and fruitful Christian married life that is centered in Christ? Conversely, do I feel as though marriage, or even dating, would interrupt the flow of my life, especially my spiritual life and relationship with Jesus? (Be honest and clear.)

4. If I am married, how does this marriage relationship enable my spouse and me—each of us and together—to stand in the place of Jesus for the good of those whose lives we touch? (Offer specific examples.)

5. If I am celibate, or at least have a sense that this may be the vocational lifestyle God has in mind for me, do I experience unusual peace in this way of life—whether I live alone or among others? How would I describe this experience of peace or quiet contentment? Am I living a celibate life primarily because it is expected or even required of me? Do I still feel open to dating? How would I describe that experience? (Be specific and honest.)

6

CAREER OR CALLING

Discerning the Difference

Whatever you do, do from the heart, as for the Lord and not for others.

Colossians 3:23

We have explored how, in the sacrament of Confirmation, you have been anointed to *be someone*—your authentic self-in-God, expressed in the vocational lifestyle that is perfectly suited to your happiness and the full flowering of your personhood. You also are anointed, in Confirmation, to *do something.* This sacramental anointing is the genesis point and animator of your vocational life now and of your eternal life-in-God. Through honest and prayerful discernment you begin to discover how God already empowers you to stand effectively in the place of the risen Lord in this time and place, in the circumstances of the life you have been given as your own.

Oftentimes I hear people say, "I just don't know what God wants me to do with my life." In fact, in times of transition the path can seem completely obscured. But such unhelpful I-just-don't-know thinking can lead to a lot of interior agitation and spiritual tail chasing. The trap lies in thinking that "where I am right now," or "what I currently do" somehow does not qualify as part of God's calling. "What I currently do" may lack the profile or even the specialness we often associate with a sense of calling.

Fortunately, discerning the ways you are best suited to be the real presence of the living Christ in your world is not beyond your reach. But where do you start?

Through prayerful observation of *patterns* of effectiveness and spiritual fruitfulness in the many areas of your life, you will begin to form a general sense of the direction in which the Holy Spirit is leading you. You will begin to glimpse what Jesus might have been pointing to when he said, "[W]hoever believes in me will do the works that I do, and will do greater ones than these" (John 14:12).

Career and Calling: Two Different Words

When it comes to the "doing" part of your Christian life, a first task is to sort out the difference between "career" and God's actual *calling* in the course of your life. Career and calling today are not necessarily the same thing. Yet only a few generations back many people spoke of their work as their calling. Their work was their profession—a word whose root points to a "declaring, avowal, or belief that leads to worthy action." There was something noble in one's giving of self, intellect, and wholehearted energy in one's work, an engagement not in personal gain or self-advancement but in service to others.

A quick tour of most any university Web site today will affirm that the focus has now shifted from calling to career, where the personal horizon is more immediate, and acquiring a marketable degree a more pressing concern. With predictable outcome, the pursuit of one's immediate horizon has trumped the long-range, deliberate discernment of that graced locus where one's talents and abilities and gifts actually intersect with the world's needs. Some people spend a lifetime climbing the career ladder, doing work which may perhaps drain them of spirit and imagination, but which offers the lure of success—or at least some promise of financial stability in uncertain times. Still, others may experience a "perfect fit" between who they are and the work they do. You might hear people who experience this right fit say something like, "I can't believe I get to do this work—and I get paid, too!" Were they just incredibly lucky? Or should the "right fit" which they experience actually be the norm for each of us, and especially for those of us who have been anointed for a purpose larger than ourselves?

How shall we describe the difference between career and calling? While the two can be the same (and in the best of all worlds they *are* the same), they carry different meanings today. Let's take a closer look at these two words.

Career comes from the word for road or racecourse. We speak of a career track, or that line of work which you pursue that promises to take you far. So the word "career" can imply "getting somewhere" in the world, advancing in responsibility, authority, recognition, and pay within your chosen field of work.[132] And that word "chosen" is important here. You *choose* a career—the one option out of many which you consider to be the most appealing and promising. When *you* choose a career, you are the active agent. The unspoken assumption here is that you possess the foresight to determine the best course to follow to get you to where *you* believe you want to go.

And that is precisely where *calling* is entirely different. Your calling in

---

[132] Interestingly, the word *career*, linked as it is to "road" or "racecourse," follows the word *careen* in my dictionary, meaning "to lurch from side to side." Many people who hurl themselves into a career in order to "get somewhere" oftentimes find themselves eventually "careening" at some point. We laughingly refer to such careening as midlife crisis.

life is not about you choosing ("My will be done"), but about the Holy Spirit leading you onto the right path of work for your life in accord with God's perfect and much larger plan ("Thy will be done"). Your calling—or more correctly, God's calling of you to a particular work of purpose and meaning in this world—also involves your *Yes* to what God already is setting in motion in your life and in the world you touch.

The difference between career and calling is the difference between "success" (which we often measure in terms of financial and material wealth) and "fruitfulness," a spiritual quality which comes about when, by grace, you "have the mind of Christ" (1 Corinthians 2:16). Here you work easily and effectively *with* the Holy Spirit in your labors and in your life. "Success" certainly is not an evil term or even a bad word. In Psalm 90 the Psalmist prays: "Give success to the work of our hands."[133] A real spiritual danger arises when success becomes self-referencing rather than a desired good that urges a person outward, enriching others in some way, or in some way revealing the unstoppable generosity and provision which are hallmarks of the reign of God.

The pursuit of success, in today's terms, can turn the human person into an efficient machine, pumping out value, sometimes seven days a week, year after year, never allowing for the necessary fallow Sabbath season, never admitting the systolic-diastolic rhythm that pulses through all of creation. Fruitfulness—and especially spiritual fruitfulness—honors the need for rest as well as for the disciplined rhythms of work. God as Creator is our first model for what human labor should look like—creative, imaginative, joyful, and

---

[133] See Psalm 90:17. This wording comes from the Grail translation found in *Christian Prayer* (stanza 9), 938. The *NAB* wording is: "Prosper the work of our hands!" In contemporary language the term *prosperity* itself can suggest a shallow, self-referencing purpose, especially in the language of "prosperity consciousness" which seemed particularly prevalent among midlevel managers who were unexpectedly "downsized" in the 1980s. Prosperity consciousness saved face and gave hope for many who were aspiring to upward mobility and who had not envisioned such an abrupt and undesired course correction in their career trajectory.

generous—followed by rest.[134]

None of this means that people who follow God's calling rather than choose for themselves a smart career will not make enough money or will never really succeed. Not at all! You can submit yourself to working wholeheartedly with the gifts, skills, and circumstances which God provides as your means to fullness of personhood, or you can run after whatever promises the gods of the marketplace are offering you today.[135] The important thing here is the focus: You can trust God's plan and pursue God's willing and God's own manner of generosity and joy of labor and rest, or you can choose what you think is going to be the best bet for your life. Quite frankly, I would rather trust God than trust my ability to chart my own course.

Jesus on "Career"

Jesus was fully aware of the pressing need, among his followers, of the basic necessities of life, and therefore he taught his followers, "[D]o not worry and say, 'What are we to eat?' or 'What are we … to wear?' … Your heavenly Father knows [what] you need . … But seek first the kingdom [of God] and his righteousness, and all these things will be given you besides" (Matthew 6:31–33). Jesus would not have said these things if they were not absolutely true. He lived these words himself, and his words carry urgent instruction and meaning

---

[134] David Whyte writes convincingly of the practical as well as the spiritual need in our work life today for this same sacred rhythm of labor and rest which renews the human spirit and allows a person to transcend the life-draining demands of career in order to reach the fruitfulness of calling. See his *Crossing the Unknown Sea,* especially chapter 9, "A Marriage with Silence: Escaping the Prison of Time and Work," and chapter 10, "Crossing the Unknown Sea: A Voyage Through the Hours of the Day."

[135] Even the question: *If I follow God's calling, will I make enough money to survive?* is a misguided question. For those who truly seek the reign of God in their life and their work, "enough" is not a bloated or endlessly and unsustainably expansive term. In the reign of God, enough is *enough,* meaning your needs will be satisfied in such quantity and quality as to fully satisfy the need, "fully and overflowing" as Jesus notes in his teaching in the Sermon on the Plain: "Give and gifts will be given to you; a good measure, packed together, shaken down, and overflowing, will be poured into your lap" (Luke 6:38).

for our lives today—especially in the shakedown of an economy based on phantom investment swaps and market speculation, a runaway economy disconnected from what the Earth can actually sustain.

Jesus does say something both surprising and challenging that we might easily overlook. *"But seek first the kingdom of God,"* he says to his disciples (v. 33). In the midst of his teaching on God's generous provision he speaks a profoundly vocational phrase, a "values" phrase which orients us toward the larger, redemptive meaning of our work. These are the words of God's calling. The phrase, "Seek first God's reign in your life," is quite different from the message which our culture would impress upon us today—"Seek first the sure path to security, the fast track to success."

Seeking first the reign of God does not necessarily mean seeking first a ministry within the church. For some, yes, but for the vast majority of God's anointed, not at all. The reign of God is everywhere, and the redemptive quality of our labors applies in all areas of human endeavor. As Jesus affirmed, the reign of God "is among you." Indeed, the reign of God "is within you."[136] You carry within yourself—within your being and your doing—the light and grace of the reign of God. It is not by chance that we find these words of Jesus situated in the context of his great teaching on a new reign-of-God way of living which begins with the Beatitudes.[137]

---

[136] In the *NAB* the phrase in Luke 17:21 is "the kingdom of God is among you," and in the *Holy Bible: New International Version* (Grand Rapids, MI: Zondervan Bible Publishers, 1973, 1996), the phrase reads, "the kingdom of God is within you." Reminiscent of this passage, twentieth century Cistercian monk and writer Thomas Merton notes, "[T]he gate of heaven is everywhere" (*Conjectures of a Guilty Bystander*, in *Thomas Merton: Spiritual Master*), 146.

[137] See Matthew 5–7. In Gerard Thomas Straub's video *The Narrow Path: Walking Toward Peace and Nonviolence with John Dear, SJ* (Burbank, CA: The San Damiano Foundation, 2007), Jesuit peace activist Fr. John Dear speaks of the Beatitudes as encouragements, by which Jesus exhorts his followers—meaning those with least power within the culture—to persist on the difficult path of virtue in order to reveal the reign of God.

The Nature of God's Calling

When your work is an expression of God's plan for your life and for the world you touch, you are actually living your vocation. This does not mean that you are doing "ultimate things," or that you have found your "forever" job. It does not even mean that you receive monetary recognition for this work. But you will be engaged, feeling wholehearted, and experiencing a joyful effectiveness, even if quietly expressed.[138]

The work you do now may not be the work you will do for the rest of your life, or even the work you will do next year. But it will express God's desiring for where you are in your life right now. Vocationally, "right now" refers to the particular relationships and commitments, circumstances and details, for which you are accountable in this time and place. Your fundamental and ongoing—indeed eternal—vocation is to life in Christ. This calling spans and links and makes sense of and gives life to the many temporal callings you will experience in the course of your life. Your anointing in the Holy Spirit remains your source of direction and your constant strength.

How can you reliably know whether you actually are following God's calling? When your work life is grounded in what you want ("my way, and now—or at least, soon!") rather than grounded in God's desiring quietly at work within you, you will find that relationship with God quickly falls off center and slips distractingly out of focus. When your work life *is* grounded in God's desiring coming to life within you, you will become like the person who finds a treasure hidden in a field, and who quickly goes and sells everything in order to buy that field. Or you will find that you are like the merchant in search of fine pearls who finds one pearl of great value and sells everything in order to buy

---

[138] Whyte speaks of vocation as being one's way of becoming visible in the world. See David Whyte, *The Three Marriages: Reimagining Work, Self and Relationship* (New York: Riverhead Books, 2009, 288.

it.[139] When your work life is grounded in God's perfect plan, you will be *on fire with the Holy Spirit,* even if quietly or in hidden ways, willing to sell all you have for the treasure of serving the reign of God. And you will ignite your world with holy possibility, as only the Spirit of the living Christ can do.

You do not need to live your life trapped in the crosscurrent between career and calling. You are anointed for a higher purpose, for a necessary work within God's plan. In Confirmation you have been anointed in the Holy Spirit to be far more bold and clear and persistent than you have yet imagined. In your life and in your work you can trust that you *will* stand in the place of the living Christ. In fact, you already do, whether you have consciously given yourself to that noble partnership or not. And you can expect to accomplish things that will make sense only by the grace of God. For those anointed in the Holy Spirit, expecting miracles should be the "new normal." Why? Because as St. Paul writes, we live no longer for ourselves "but for him who for [our] sake died and was raised" (2 Corinthians 5:15). By the grace of God you already are giving your *Yes* to the perfection of God's eternal plan which uniquely includes *you.* Already you are putting your heart with God for the next phase of your life's trajectory, whether you think you are doing that adequately or not, and even though you cannot know for certain where "putting your heart with God" will take you.

How can you be sure that you are following God's plan for your life? *You will never know God's plan with absolute vocational certainty.* Respecting the mystery of God and walking steadfast and humbly in faith, and listening with the ear of the heart, will aid your lifelong discernment of God's perfect willing for your life.

---

[139] See Matthew 13:44–46. In these two brief parables—three sentences total—Jesus calls his listeners' attention to the vocational merit of these enterprising endeavors in the transactions of commerce. These merchants are not "getting something for nothing." Rather, they sell *all they have.* They are as fully invested in *their* lives as Jesus is invested in *our* lives.

Five Steps to Discern Your Calling

Your ongoing discernment of God's willing for your life need not be complex. This discernment is not a one-time project, nor is it a discernment of "ultimate things" such as the way of life or the kind of work that you imagine will engage you for the rest of your life. Your lifelong discernment concerns the humble cluster of relationships, commitments, circumstances, insights, needs, and opportunities which shape your life, not by chance or intention but by the graced choreography of the Holy Spirit.[140] Discernment of God's calling requires your wholehearted engagement in the reign of God as you encounter it here, at this time, supported by some faithful and consistent steps on your part. Discerning God's willing requires lifelong faithfulness and loving obedience as God's plan unfolds over time, through all the changing circumstances of your life. So you will find yourself repeating these five steps often—and in some circumstances, even daily.[141]

Step 1: *Prayerfully open yourself to God's perfect plan.* There is a world of difference between generally feeling that you are open to whatever God wants in your life, and placing yourself in the spiritually vulnerable position of handing over the car keys, so to speak, and buckling yourself into the passenger seat of your own car which now is being driven by the sometimes wild Mystery of God.[142] If the only thing you do each day in your morning prayer is to open yourself with complete trust and intentionality to God's desiring, and to the unforeseen exquisite movement of the Holy Spirit in your life this day, that will be a good and worthy morning prayer.[143] Intentionally expressing complete trust

---

[140] I have encountered several people who, *because of* loss of a parent or sibling to disease, have pursued an unexpected yet fruitful calling in medical research, patient care, or patient advocacy.

[141] More resources for personal vocational discernment can be found at the Awakening Vocations Web site, http://www.awakeningvocations.com. Resources to discern spiritual gifts, or charisms, are available at the Catherine of Siena Institute Web site, http://www.siena.org.

[142] I once saw a bumper sticker that read: "If God is your co–pilot, change seats immediately!"—an important and oftentimes challenging vocational wisdom.

[143] As the Christian man or woman matures, more substantial prayer is required to sustain the soul, to develop conscience for ever greater identification with Christ, and to expand capacity to bring the concerns of the world into the circle of divine compassion and creative response. I encourage people

in—and cooperation with—God's wisdom, love, and provision is an honest, powerful, and spiritually liberating act at the start of your day. But note: This is not about asking God to bless *your* plans, but asking God to use you according to *God's* plans, which carry their own blessing. The difference here is crucial and even startling. Praying honestly not for *my* will but *Thy* will can be a lifelong conversional struggle. For this reason Jesus repeatedly insisted of his followers: "Do *not* be afraid."[144] Absolute trust in God is a vocational imperative.

Step 2: *Notice things.* Having prayerfully opened yourself to God's movement, expect that things which are either immediate in your life or on the more distant horizon will begin to shift. It is important to be mentally, emotionally, and spiritually present enough to your life to notice what is happening. Most people within our culture today are tuned in to something that is worlds removed from their surroundings. We have grown accustomed to living our separate lives in our plugged-in, downloadable, app-saturated, on-demand universes. We are here but not really.[145] But when you are working with God you have to *be here now*. Being here now is the lived affirmation of the centrality of the Incarnation in Christian life. Being here now means dialing down the noise and the chatter, letting go the mindless conversations, the tweets, and the endless empty distractions, stepping away from the relentless

---

who take God's calling in their life seriously to pray the Liturgy of the Hours—not because it conveniently fits their busy schedule (it never does) but because this expression of liturgical prayer gives rhythm and discipline to the concerns and endeavors of human life, centering heart, mind, and imagination in the work of the dying and the rising which defines the paschal mystery lived out in daily experience.

[144] While Jesus admonishes his followers with this phrase approximately seventeen times in the Gospels, the two most poignant and challenging instances can be found at Matthew 14:27, when Jesus approaches the apostles adrift in the storm-tossed boat and says, "Take courage, it is I; do not be afraid," and then invites Peter to come to him across the water; and at Matthew 28:10, when the risen Lord says to the women at the empty tomb, "Do not be afraid. Go tell my brothers to go to Galilee, and there they will see me." He admonishes them, in essence, to not be afraid of the totally new thing that is happening: the inbreaking of the reign of God in human life and circumstance.

[145] Over forty years ago songwriter Paul Simon perhaps anticipated this existential vacancy in these words: "Half of the time we're gone and we don't know where / And we don't know where." Paul Simon, "The Only Living Boy in New York," *Simon and Garfunkel: Bridge Over Troubled Water* (New York: Columbia/Legacy, 88697 82724 2, 2010) (originally recorded November 15, 1969).

overstimulation and the "brain vegging."

Why? Because you have been anointed to stand, in *this* time and in *these* circumstances, in the place of the living Christ for the work of revealing the reign of God. Notice what's going on right in front of you, around you, inside you. The still small voice of the Holy Spirit does not stand a chance of being heard in the overstimulated world we inhabit today. But by virtue of your anointing you possess the power to give the Holy Spirit the interior space to move into action. Notice what you hear and what you see. Notice circumstances and any unexpected subtle changes in tone in the larger conversation between your inner self and the world. Notice what you hear or read in the news, and notice how you respond to it.

Notice what in the world—in your world or in the larger world—is going on; notice what breaks your heart, and therefore breaks the heart of God. Notice what it is like for you, spiritually, to "feel as God feels in this world."[146] Notice the opportunities that open to you, as well as the opportunities that are taken from you, or that dry up, or that simply never arrive. Notice your immediate gut reactions and feelings, and notice how you finally respond.[147] The work at this stage of discerning God's calling is to pay attention. Be here now, where God already is at work and where Jesus is waiting to reveal an unexpected path in order to touch the world through you.

Step 3: *Take action.* Noticing things is your *call* to action. But the moment when you actually begin to take action or initiative, in a sense, sets

---

[146] Ronald Rolheiser, in his book *The Holy Longing: The Search for a Christian Spirituality* (New York: Doubleday, 1999), writes compellingly of "how God feels in this world, and how Jesus felt on Good Friday" (186–7).

[147] In recent years, for example, I have encountered many married couples who discover that they are unable to conceive and bring forth children. In each instance there is a grieving over a long-cherished opportunity that seems to elude them, then dries up; and eventually the couple acknowledges that the opportunity will never arrive. The deeper work of God's calling—that deeper vocational work—requires a courageous noticing of present circumstances and honest acceptance before next steps can be taken. A helpful question here is: *Did God make a mistake?* The question deserves open conversation, honest answers, and a willingness to explore what God might have in mind within, say, the life of *this* marriage, or within *these* unanticipated circumstances.

God's gears in motion. God is always inviting you, encouraging your initiative, urging and guiding your participation and your wholehearted partnership in the work of redemption.

Develop the habit of recognizing opportunities to use the gifts God has given you. Gravitate toward whatever animates your heart and mind and swings you into action. Recognize those particular circumstances when your gifts and talents seem to connect effortlessly, effectively, and in some graced way, with the situation at hand. Develop confidence in walking through the doors that are opened to you by the Holy Spirit; respond to the people placed in your path who will give you the next piece you need for the work you have to do. Give it a try; take action. Let go your grip and get out of the boat; fix your eyes on Jesus who invites you, and put one foot in front of the other. Bend your knees, breathe, and move forward.

Step 4: *Prayerfully examine the results.* The human person possesses a unique capacity to reflect upon circumstance and experience in a way that produces meaning, a sense of purpose and direction; and equally possesses the capacity to act further in an integrative way. These human capacities play an important role in discerning patterns of God's movement within and through your life.

As you prayerfully reflect on your experience and examine the outcomes of your actions, you can ask yourself these helpful questions: Were others touched in some positive way by my presence and my actions? Did I feel led by the Holy Spirit? What was that experience like? Did my presence and my actions give evidence, even in some small way, of my faith and trust in God and my confidence in what I was doing? How did I feel in the moment? Was I energized? engaged? able to be really present?

Be spiritually honest with yourself as you answer these questions. Ask Jesus what *he* thinks about your experience and its outcomes. Ask him what *he* thinks about the way you are living your life. This prayerful examination of results actually has a technical name. It is called theological reflection, which brings your lived experience into prayerful and dynamic conversation with the Scriptures and the church's heritage and teaching.[148]

You will not be successful at everything you do nor with every initiative you undertake. It is good to acknowledge your limitations up front. But in some situations, in some of your endeavors, you may rightly be amazed and encouraged with how effective you are, and how effective the Holy Spirit is within you, without undue effort on your part. Bring your reflection on your experience into conversation with a trusted other—your pastor, a wise elder or mentor, a spiritual director, or vocational guide.[149]

Step 5: *Take the next obvious step.* After you have prayerfully examined the results of your efforts, do the next obvious thing. This might mean making a suggested phone call, researching resources online, making an appointment for the next key conversation, or enrolling in a course of studies. In some situations, doing the next obvious thing might mean continuing, for now, in a job that you have outgrown or that does not fit right, quietly confident that the Holy Spirit already is setting in motion the next pieces that need to come into place. Sometimes, if you feel stuck and do not know what to do next, "the next obvious thing" might mean doing household chores, sweeping the porch, running errands, checking in on an elderly neighbor, going for a walk. The point is: *Do something.* Get away from whatever you are hovering over (like the phone which does not ring, or the empty mailbox, or the résumé or research paper which you cannot seem to write). Give God space to be GOD in this situation. Stay faithful. Trust. Let God's simple joy and the consolation of God's

---

[148] See Killen and De Beer, *The Art of Theological Reflection.* See also my *Moving in God's Direction,* chap. 11.

[149] The fourth and final step of the Awakening Vocations process (http://www.awakeningvocations .com/awakeningvocations.html) trains individuals within parishes who are gifted in these mentoring ways to be parish-based vocational guides for parishioners through every age and state in life.

abiding friendship sustain you.[150]

Discerning God's calling, and growing in partnership with the Holy Spirit, is a lifelong process. It is the path of vocational joy. Legend has it that St. Catherine of Siena once said, "All the way to heaven is heaven, for Jesus said, 'I am the way.'" When you honestly and deeply accept your anointing in the Holy Spirit you cannot fall off the path, and ultimately you cannot lose your way. God has invested too dearly in you to let that happen.

You are anointed for a purpose. Is it to do a particular job? It may be. You can trust that a life of faithfulness and obedience, wholehearted application of your gifts and talents, and quiet satisfaction in work well done may be your particular gift to your world. But knowing what we do know of God, you may be called upon to accomplish what you have not yet imagined.

What God wants to give this world, more than anything else, is peace, which is the ultimate expression of blessedness within the reign of God.[151] Peacemaking in today's war-torn world requires actual peacemakers—men and women anointed to stand in the breach of discord in the cause of peace. Next we will look at the centrality of peace in Jesus' life and teaching, and explore why peacemaking is an integral part of your particular vocational work of love as God's anointed one living in the twenty-first century.

---

[150] I write here from experience. In my mid-fifties (not a highly employable age, I discovered) and suddenly unemployed in a saturated church lay ministry market, I worked the broader job market hard, on and off, for eighteen months. I noticed that during the "off" spells I felt at peace, creative, and energized by projects of my own. When I finally let go the illusion that there was a full-time job "out there" with my name on it, I was free to enter into God's dream for my life. These five steps to discerning God's calling have proven themselves worthy.

[151] See Jesus' inaugural teaching of the Beatitude life in Matthew 5:3–12, especially v. 9. See also John 14:27: "Not as the world gives [peace] do I give it to you."

Questions for Conversation

1. What two or three points can I glean from this chapter?

2. In what areas of my life might I be praying: *"My* will be done"? In my prayer, am I trying hard to get God to see a stuck situation from my perspective? What *am* I really praying for? (Be specific.)

3. If I feel vocationally at a stuck point, what is that stuckness like for me? How would I describe it? (Be specific.) What am I doing about it? What results am I getting? (Again, be specific.) What might I do, or do differently, to become unstuck? What is my timeline or action plan to become free of this stuck place?

4. How do I feel when I honestly pray: *"Thy* will be done"? Do I feel insincere? terrified? liberated? hopeful? (Be specific.)

7

ANOINTED FOR PEACEMAKING

Why Peace Defines the Core of Christian Life

Blessed are the peacemakers, for they will be called children of
God.

Matthew 5:9

If we look at the Gospels, and closely examine the words and actions
and the way of life of this man Jesus, what seems to have mattered most to him?
What formed the core of his life and shaped his earthly ministry? How might we
describe his mission? Even a quick look in the Gospels at the teachings of Jesus
reveals something interesting about the words he focused on in his public
preaching and in the more intimate teachings among his inner circle of
followers.

According to Strong's *Concordance,* in the Gospel accounts Jesus mentions the word *love* forty-three times.[152] We would expect love to be preeminent in the vocabulary of Jesus' teachings. He uses the word *forgiveness* in its various forms forty times; and we would expect this, too, from the One who came "to reconcile all things for [God]."[153] Jesus uses the word *faith* twenty-six times, often in the context of admonishment, as in "O you of little faith."[154] He uses the word *peace* twenty-six times.[155] *Trust,* which can be understood as either faith or hope, appears among Jesus' words three times. Interestingly, according to Strong's *Concordance,* Jesus uses the word *hope* only once.[156] (Hope, however, appears forty times in the letters of St. Paul.)

Setting the Context for Peacemaking

The preeminent teaching on peacemaking in the New Testament can be found in Jesus' inaugural teaching on life as it is lived within the reign of God.[157] In the Beatitudes presented in St. Matthew's Gospel, Jesus instructs his followers: "Blessed are the peacemakers, / for they will be called children of God" (Matthew 5:9).

And who were his followers? They were not U.N. diplomats, nor even regional heads of state. They were neither titans of industry nor household-name CEOs. His followers were not the movers and shakers nor the cultural icons of

---

[152] Strong, *Concordance,* s.v. "Love."

[153] Ibid., s.v. "Forgiveness." See Colossians 1:19–20a: "For in him all the fullness was pleased to dwell, / and through him to reconcile all things for him, / making peace by the blood of his cross." Note here that the fulfillment of this work of reconciliation is the "making [of] peace."

[154] Strong, *Concordance,* s.v. "Faith." See, for example, Matthew 6:30, where Jesus chides his followers for not trusting in God's love and provision for them as fully as God cares for the birds of the air, the wild flowers, and the grass of the fields. Jesus' admonishment is harder to take when the apostles' little boat is getting tossed about on a stormy sea and they believe they are about to perish (see Matthew 8:26).

[155] Strong, *Concordance,* s.v. "Peace."

[156] Ibid., s.v. "Hope."

[157] See Matthew 5:3–12. In St. Luke's Gospel, the Sermon on the Plain (Luke 6:20–49, esp. vv. 20–26) presents only a sketch of Matthew's fuller list. The Lucan account balances four statements of beatitude with four statements of woe.

his day. Jesus' followers were not recognized influencers of any sort. His followers were the *anawim*—the landless poor, the marginalized, the uneducated, the powerless, the ones with no standing in society and no one to lobby on behalf of their concerns or to speak out for the cause of their grievances. They were what some might unthinkingly dismiss as "riffraff." Yet these were the ones toward whom Jesus gravitated, the ones to whom Jesus taught the ways of blessedness and the fruits of God's faithfulness. He shared with them the good news of their rightful place in the reign of God, of sure consolation, divine inheritance, the favor of God's righteousness, divine mercy, and protection in times of persecution. In short, Jesus assured God's love and provision to those who understood all too well that "the help of man is vain."[158] Of course they would want to follow Jesus. The power of Empire was not on their side; in fact, it actively worked against them. Jesus was the one who finally could speak to their isolation, their powerlessness, and their needs in a way that gave them strength of heart.

Yet the Beatitudes, on closer reading, are interactive, dialogical, requiring human engagement for the full experience of the blessing. Of these eight encouragements, the latter four speak of the blessings that flow from actually *living a life reflective of God's covenant love.* "Be merciful," Jesus says (the fifth beatitude), "be clean of heart" (the sixth)—words which penetrate like burning exhortations down into the countless ways we humans navigate through a complex and challenging world. And now comes a distinctly higher threshold for discipleship: "Blessed are the peacemakers," Jesus exhorts (the seventh beatitude), "for they will be called children of God."

What does it mean to be powerless yet also a peacemaker? What peacemaking authority could the *anawim* ever possibly bring to situations where peace is absent? How can they possibly stand for justice and peace when they

---

[158] See Psalm 108:13. This wording comes from the Grail translation in *Christian Prayer* (959, stanza 6); the *NAB* reads: "worthless is human help." Given that women and the marginalized lacked political voice in the culture of Jesus' time, the *anawim* would have understood the full impact of this male–focused phrase.

themselves may be the targets of violence and wanton disrespect? They are the dispossessed who have no one to turn to but God, no power they can count on but God's power, no justice but God's justice to plead their cause—and that's the point. This is what Jesus wants them to understand. Relationship with God and living a life of virtue is their sure defense against caving in to the power machine that will simply chew them up and spit them out. On another occasion we find Jesus rejoicing because what God has kept hidden "from the wise and the learned you have revealed … to the childlike" (Luke 10:21). The childlike, for Jesus, were not "the adorable ones" as toddlers are often regarded today; rather, the childlike were the adults as well as children, annoying and bothersome, who had no means to add value or buy in to social respectability, or to gain social or legal standing in the culture. The "childlike" were permanently deprived of their inherent human dignity.

"Blessed are the peacemakers" is a blessing, yes, but in the light now of divine relationship peacemaking becomes much more: a responsibility, an assignment, a work to be done by those who enjoy God's protection. With these words the poor and the powerless now have a place and a purpose in life. Peacemaking now becomes in a very real sense a vocational imperative, and a particular manifestation of one's calling into divine partnership in the work of revealing the reign of God, even and especially in the places of marginality and hopelessness, hostility and injustice.

This was not Jesus' only teaching on peacemaking. His every act of forgiveness[159] and every teaching on forgiveness[160] culminated in his own forgiveness of all who took part in his execution, with his words of generous and sobering love: "Father, forgive them, they know not what they do" (Luke 23:34). Every act of forgiveness is a participation in divine peacemaking, a

---

[159] See, for example, Matthew 9:2–8 (parallels in Mark 2:3–12 and Luke 5:18–26), Jesus' healing of the paralytic man; and John 8:3–11, Jesus' encounter with the woman caught in adultery.

[160] See, for example, Matthew 6:9–15 (parallel in Luke 11:2–4), Jesus' teaching on the Lord's Prayer; and Matthew 18:21–35, the parable of the unforgiving servant.

standing in the breach to mend what is broken, as Jesus demonstrated and as St. Paul notes: "For [Christ Jesus] is our peace, he who made both one and broke down the dividing wall of enmity, through his flesh, ... that he might create in himself one new person in place of the two, thus establishing peace" (Ephesians 2:14–15). Every effort toward peacemaking insists upon and affirms the dignity of innocent blood shed and human spirit crushed by violence and blind neglect.

Peacemaking lies at the core of restorative justice, returning to wholeness what has been violently rent apart. As Jesuit peace activist Fr. John Dear notes, peacemaking is both an inner journey of conversion and a public journey of speaking the truth, resisting evil, standing with the poor, disarming the world, and creating space for the dignity of every one. For the peacemaker, Dear insists, nonviolence "is the key to understanding Jesus."[161]

Love, Forgiveness, Faith, Peace

If we take a look at the word *love,* as Jesus used it, what do we find? Jesus' teachings did not address "romantic love"—that genre of love we most quickly associate with the word today. Nor did Jesus present a teaching on an idealized platonic love or any generalized notion of love removed from real human experience. He talked about love which is *right relationship* between self, God, and neighbor.[162] He talked about love which is justice,[163] love which is the outpouring of self for the good of the other.[164] He taught very specifically,

---

[161] John Dear, SJ, *Living Peace: A Spirituality of Contemplation and Action* (New York: Image Doubleday, 2001), 85.

[162] See Jesus' teaching on the Greatest Commandment (love of God), which he links to a second commandment "[which] is like it" (love of neighbor) (see Matthew 22:37–39; see also Mark 12:29–31, and Luke 10:25–28 where the scholar of the law gives the answer to his own question). The authority of Jesus' teaching was that in his life and in the self-offering of his passion and death he fully and redemptively lived the commandments he taught.

[163] See the preeminent teaching in Jesus' parable of the Judgment of the Nations (Matthew 25:31–46, esp. vv. 31–40).

[164] See the parable of the Good Samaritan (Luke 10:29–37); and the parable of the Lost Son (Luke 15:11–32).

very clearly, and repeatedly, about love of enemies,[165] love that disarms the will to war and brings reconciliation instead.[166] Love, Jesus showed us, is at the service of peace. Even in his midnight mock trial and receiving a sentence of death, Jesus the nonviolent One did not counter violence with violence but rather, held fast in silence and peace.

For Jesus, "holding fast in peace" is the costly expression of that love which defines the reign of God. It will take you and me a lifetime and more to really understand what Jesus was teaching when he spoke about love and taught about peace.

When Jesus used the word *forgiveness* (or *forgive,* or *forgiven*), he meant it as an unexplainable release from bondage, an unmerited release from debt, a graced release from the interior and relational havoc wreaked by the violence of sin and moral oppression. Interestingly, in the accounts of some of Jesus' healings we find that physical healing occurred instantaneously in his forgiveness of the debt of sin.[167] For Jesus, forgiveness is the breaking of the shackles of beholdenness to the sway of moral, relational, and social violence.[168] Forgiveness closes the chasm between life and death, mends the division between life at the center and half-life at the margins. Such healing through forgiveness creates a pathway to peace, which is the restoration of divine right order for one's wholehearted participation in life.

When Jesus used the word *faith,* he was talking really about an

---

[165] Again, see the parable of the Good Samaritan (Luke 10:29–37); Samaritans were the hated foreigners. See also Jesus' teachings directly focused on love of enemies (e.g., Matthew 5:43–48; Luke 6:27–36).

[166] A preeminent example is in Jesus' healing the severed ear of the servant of the high priest at the scene of his arrest (Luke 22:50–51).

[167] See Jesus' healing of the paralytic (Matthew 9:1–8; Mark 2:1–12; Luke 5:17–26). In the healing of the Gerasene demoniac (Mark 5:1–20) Jesus does not expressly "forgive sin" but liberates the tortured man from the shackles of "an unclean spirit" (v. 2).

[168] See the spiritual and social restoration of the woman caught in adultery (John 8:3–11), and of the woman who anointed Jesus' feet (Luke 7:36–50). We can only wonder what psychological and moral healing might have occurred in those involved in Jesus' execution, for whom Jesus prayed, "Father, forgive them, they know not what they do" (Luke 23:34).

absolute, unwavering trust in God, strong enough to bear the weight of human concern and human grief, a radical trust which has a liberating effect on the human spirit. Jesus spoke with authority when he spoke of faith because his own relationship with his Father was one of open trust, and complete and total dependence on the love, provision, and protection of his Abba.[169] Jesus understood and embraced something that most of us, most of the time, would rather ignore: humankind's absolute poverty apart from God. When Jesus spoke phrases like "Have faith in God and faith in me," he meant, in essence, *The Father and I are your safety net. So step forward fearlessly and in so doing reveal the reign of God.* True, Jesus readily meets us where we are, in our places of helplessness and even hopelessness. But he also wants to meet us where *he* is, in the new reality of Resurrection life, even if it means overriding the physical laws of nature, as with Peter whom Jesus invited to step out of the boat and into the storm.[170]

What might Jesus' words mean for your life today? When he speaks of faith he is saying to you: *As God's anointed one, show your absolute trust in me by doing what only the Holy Spirit can accomplish.* And what work does the Holy Spirit desire to accomplish in you and through you? Ultimately it is restoration of right relationship of yourself with God, with others, and with all creation. This brings us to the heart of the meaning of redemption—to be purchased back, restored to original dignity and worth. God's work in you and through you eventually brings your world, the world you touch, from disharmony to harmony, from war to peace, from the disorienting spin of chaos

---

[169] See, for example, John 11:41–42, the raising of Lazarus, where Jesus prays, "Father, I thank you for hearing me. I know that you always hear me; but because of the crowd here I have said this, that they may believe that you sent me." When his own life hung in the balance, Jesus abandoned himself to his Father's willing. See Mark 14:36: "Abba, Father, all things are possible to you. Take this cup away from me, but not what I will but what you will" (see also Matthew 26:39; Luke 22:42).

[170] See Jesus' consoling word to his closest followers on the night before his arrest: "In my Father's house there are many dwelling places. ... I will come back again and take you to myself, so that *where I am you also may be*" (John 14:2–3, emphasis added). See also Matthew 14:22–33, the account of Jesus walking on the water, especially vv. 27–29, where Jesus says, "Take courage, it is I; do not be afraid." In an interior leap of faith, Peter says, "Lord, if it is you, command me to come to you on the water." And Jesus replies simply: "Come." Peter gets out of the boat and, overriding the physical laws of nature by an act of faith in Jesus, begins to walk on the water.

to right order and the full flowering of your personhood-in-God. Faith, or absolute trust in God, is always at the service of peace.

So let's take a look at this word *peace*. Unsurprisingly, in Jesus' inaugural teaching on the Beatitudes, "Blessed are the peacemakers" was not the first of the beatitudes but the seventh. This does not mean that peacemaking ranks lower on the list or is tucked in as an afterthought. Rather, being poor in spirit, mourning what needs to be mourned, being meek and not pushy, hungering and thirsting for God's righteousness, being merciful and pure of heart, all are prerequisites, conversion points on the way to peacemaking, the preeminent expression and evidence of the reign of God. And in being a peacemaker, Jesus cautioned, you can count on persecution, but you also can count on inheriting nothing less than the reign of God.

Peacemaking held a preeminent place in Jesus' attitude and actions as well as in his teaching. In the Garden of Gethsemane at the scene of his arrest, at the most vulnerable moment of his public life, Jesus, armed only with a burning desire to do his Father's willing, touched and healed the soldier whose ear had been severed by a sword, and spoke a stinging word about arming oneself against violence.[171] On the cross, Jesus brought the divine kiss of peace to the criminal who acknowledged him as Messiah.[172] And in St. John's Gospel, Jesus' first words to the Apostles gathered in the upper room on the morning of his resurrection were: *Peace be with you.* He showed them his hands and his side, and then he said to them a second time: *Peace be with you.* Jesus then breathed on the Apostles and said to them, "Receive the holy Spirit. Whose sins you forgive are forgiven them, and whose sins you retain are retained."[173] Of all the things Jesus could have said upon rising from the dead, the Scriptures tell us that

---

[171] See Matthew 26:51–52. St. Matthew records that "one of those who accompanied Jesus" pulled out his sword and struck off the high priest's servant's ear, and Jesus responded, "Put your sword back into its sheath, for all who take the sword will perish by the sword." In St. John's Gospel (18:10–11), the one with the sword was Peter.

[172] See Luke 23:43.

[173] See John 20:19–23. Here Jesus distinctly gives to the Apostles the unique authority (to forgive sins) which revealed his own divine origins and which became the cause of his arrest and execution.

words of peace were the words he shared first. These most beautiful words were powerful enough to unlock the Apostles from their fear, opening them to receive Jesus' breathing forth of the Holy Spirit. "Peace" is not one among many words but the preeminent word which defines restoration and harmony within the reign of God and sets the work of redemption into motion.

Peacemaking in the Life of the Church

The church from the earliest days understood the preeminence of this gift of peace and the deep conversional quality of the practice of peacemaking. In Jesus' teachings expressed in the catechesis of the early church, the public avowal of peace—especially by those undergoing conversion from a life sworn to arms in the Roman military—was the sure sign of conversion.[174] A soldier could bear arms, or conversely could forswear the military life and stand for peace, but he could not do both. In fact, a person undergoing conversion was required to let go even a warring spirit in order to hear and take to heart the church's teachings of peace.

In the early church a life of peacemaking and active nonviolence also was an effective form of evangelizing. The Gospel spread not only through words but through attitude, actions, and a consistent Christ-centered way of life (even to the point of risking one's life "for the sake of the name").[175] And that way of life flowed from the gift of peace of the risen Christ. The steadfast nonviolence of the early followers who were tortured and thrown as raw meat to

---

[174] See Alan F. Kreider, "Learning to Live like Christians," *The Sign of Peace,* Spring 2010, 21–24. This quarterly publication of the Catholic Peace Fellowship (http://www.catholicpeacefellowship .org) began in 1965 under the inspiration and guidance of such peace activists as Thomas Merton, Dorothy Day, and Philip and Daniel Berrigan. The organization's mission is to "support Catholic conscientious objectors through education, counseling, and advocacy."

[175] See Acts 5:28–40, where the high priest questioned the Apostles, "We gave you strict orders [did we not?] to stop teaching in that name," and after receiving a flogging, the Apostles again were ordered to not teach in the name of Jesus. St. Luke writes, "So they left the presence of the Sanhedrin, rejoicing that they had been found worthy to suffer dishonor for the sake of the name" (v. 41).

hungry lions became unnerving to their persecutors, some of whom converted to the faith because of the witness of these early Christians to the redemptive power of nonviolence and peace.[176] Early followers were catechists (echoers of the faith) by virtue of their steadfast nonviolent way of life, a life deeply formed by the steadfast witness of Jesus, the preeminently nonviolent and nail-scarred One. Following Jesus' resurrection, Thomas, one of the Eleven, went so far as to declare that only this nail-scarred One was worthy of his confession of faith, "My Lord and my God," and the only One worth following.[177]

The preeminence of Jesus' peacemaking finds expression in the church's worship today. Understood in all the Eucharistic Prayers and stated explicitly in the intimate liturgical language of Eucharistic Prayer III of the recently retired 1985 edition of the Roman Missal is the very purpose of Jesus' life, death, and resurrection: "Lord, may this sacrifice, *which has made our peace with you,* advance the peace and salvation of all the world."[178] Similar in tone, the 2011 translation reads: "May this Sacrifice of our reconciliation, we pray, O Lord, advance the peace and salvation of all the world."[179] In the 1985 Eucharistic Prayer I for Masses of Reconciliation, Jesus is described as "our Passover and our lasting peace." (The 2011 translation reads: "our Passover and our surest peace.") And in the 1985 Eucharistic Prayer II for Masses of Reconciliation we recall that it is God's own Spirit who "changes … hearts" so that "nations [may] seek the way of peace together." (The new translation reads, "[Y]ou change our hearts to prepare them for reconciliation.") Reconciliation and peace go hand in hand in our work of revealing the reign of God.

---

[176] See Kreider, "Learning to Live like Christians," 22.

[177] See John 20:28. In this passage Thomas is usually regarded as a doubter or "weak in faith." In fact, I believe he is telegraphing an important message to the community of believers—a message that applies equally today: "If the one you follow cannot produce the scars that testify to a redeeming God, then that one is not worth following." Many people in our culture today acknowledge and even revere Jesus as a great and worthy prophet and teacher, but for them the cross remains a stumbling block and a sign of foolishness, as St. Paul warned it would (see 1 Corinthians 1:23).

[178] *The Roman Missal, Second Edition* (New York: Catholic Book Publishing, 1985), Eucharistic Prayer III (emphasis added).

[179] *The Roman Missal, Third Edition* (Washington, DC: ICEL, 2010), Eucharistic Prayer III.

Anointed for Peacemaking

What wisdom can the early church's witness of peace speak to our lives in our well-armed and hypervigilant twenty-first century world? Carrying a handgun is considered smart protection. National defense spending—from the search for possibilities of war to preparedness for war, to engagement in war and cleaning up the aftermath—has a price tag that fiscally we cannot calculate and morally we cannot face. Readiness to inflict the preemptive strike, whether through active firepower or through robotically controlled drones, whether in proactive self-defense or to protect national security or access to critical resources, is considered prudent and proactive policy. In our trigger-ready culture, a show of violence—or at least the display of capacity for violence—secures bragging rights to a frightening brand of superiority.

But what impact does a culture's readiness for violence have on the soul of a nation? How does this readiness for violence shape the church's own conversation with the world in which it is situated? How does our culture's readiness for violence shape the ways in which you and I engage in our part of this twenty-first century world? Intentional peacemaking must be a clear moral value which we bring to all of our relationships and dealings with others. Actual intentional peacemaking—not backed up with swords—also must be the consistent moral value which we insist upon in our nation's leaders. This stance of peacemaking is quite different from "not making waves." And, far from being a sign of weakness or capitulation, peacemaking demands spiritual strength and a singular moral focus. Peacemaking lies at the heart of Christian faith because it animates the very pulse of justice and life within the human community.

Because we are anointed in the Holy Spirit, the concerns of a world trapped in the vortex of violence will touch us as long as we live. Eventually these concerns will become our concerns, because we cannot separate ourselves from the web of all living things, nor hermetically seal ourselves off from the moral anguish of the world's soul.

Even if we were to subscribe to the practical rationale for self-protection or national security, no matter the cost, a certain restlessness for right relationship with God, self, others, and the world will tell us that being armed against violence can never lead to peace.[180] In fact, being armed against violence is a setup for violence, as Jesus sternly warned at the scene of his own arrest.[181] He was and remains the living expression of a peace that needs no weapons to defend it. Such divine peace is incapable of aggression or retaliation—a truth that speaks a sobering challenge for our lives today. Every one of us is anointed for a purpose far more serious and self-involving than we may wish to acknowledge, and the Holy Spirit will not let us go—nor abandon us—until that purpose is fulfilled. Every one of us is anointed to stand in some intentional way in the place of Jesus, the preeminently nonviolent One, and therefore we arm ourselves at our own peril.

By virtue of our anointed life in Christ, the Holy Spirit is at work to awaken each of us to that steadfast way of peace which defines us uniquely as followers of Jesus the nonviolent One, and shapes our lives as fresh expressions of Jesus' living presence today. You might be the peacemaker within your immediate or extended family, and able to heal wounds spanning many generations. You might be the one who can defuse hostile situations in the workplace, in public places, or in the broader community. Or you might be called upon to mediate peace between hostile groups or organizations, or even between nations.[182]

---

[180] St. John's Gospel, especially chapter 13 and onward, makes the point that "power over" and "communion with" cannot abide together. War generates war; peace generates peace.

[181] See Matthew 26:52 regarding use of the sword.

[182] Occasionally diplomats emerge on the world stage who break deadlocks between warring nations or factions within a nation. One example was Dag Hammarksjöld, second Secretary General of the United Nations, a tireless negotiator for peace between nations and for release of prisoners of war. Another, former Senator George Mitchell, has helped to forge peace treaties in Ireland and in Middle East countries. Groups of women also have rallied fearlessly as peacemakers, peace educators, and frontline advocates for peace in countries such as Rwanda and Liberia, and become peace formators

St. Paul ardently urged the early Christian community which was undergoing persecution: "Have no anxiety at all, but in everything, by prayer and petition, with thanksgiving, make your requests known to God. Then the peace of God that surpasses all understanding will guard your hearts and minds in Christ Jesus" (Philippians 4:6–7). Being a steadfast and intentional peacemaker in an armed and violent world is a preeminent dimension of what it means to be anointed for a purpose and conformed to Christ in the twenty-first century.

Peacemaking and Conscience

Achieving mature stature as a peacemaker, the Beatitudes insist, is the necessary work in becoming a son or daughter of God.[183] It is not easy work— far from it. Peacemaking is intentional work, putting your will with God's perfect willing in vulnerable situations. And peacemaking is costly work, putting your life, your name and reputation, even your immediate physical safety, in the gap where conflict holds sway, assured that ultimately, "all things hold together in Christ."[184] Formation of *personal* conscience, so critical to expression of mature Christian faith, is grounded in this ethic of peacemaking—of being disarmed first of all in attitude, servant-hearted in relationship with God, and therefore disarmed and servant-hearted in relationship with others.

And as you vocationally mature in the Holy Spirit you experience the awakening of *social* conscience as well, which turns you outward with the eyes

---

between Palestine and Israel, and Northern Ireland and the Republic of Ireland. In the United States, poet activist and former gang member Luis Rodrigues travels and speaks nationwide, training educators, law enforcement officers, prison personnel, and gang leaders in nonviolent ways of defusing gang culture. No matter one's faith or belief system, the Christian claim is that there is no peace and no peacemaking apart from the peace of the risen Christ. See Ephesians 1:9–10, extolling the Father's plan of salvation "set forth in [Christ] as a plan for the fullness of times, to sum up all things in Christ, in heaven and on earth."

[183] See Matthew 5:9.

[184] See Colossians 1:17.

and mind and heart of Christ Jesus to address the wider expressions of injustice and violence in our world. If you are willing to give your Yes to God, the Holy Spirit's passion for peacemaking *will* conform your heart to the heart of Christ, so that you can courageously, imaginatively, and compassionately intersect the world's anguish and the world's longing with God's redeeming love, according to the ways you have been gifted.

This, ultimately, is the purpose of your anointing: to stand in the place of the living Christ with grace and authority, and in his name to advocate and press forward for the cause of life and justice and mercy and peace in this twenty-first century world which God still so loves.

Questions for Conversation

1. What two or three points can I glean from this chapter?

2. In what situations in my life is it simply easier for me to resort to violence—in attitude, words, or actions—than to restrain and calm myself with nonviolence? Do I create or respond to conflict with polite but passive forms of aggression? For me, what is the payoff in these situations? (Be specific.)

3. When I intentionally choose nonviolence in my attitude, words, or actions, how do I feel—spiritually, emotionally, physically? (Give examples; be specific.)

4. In my immediate world, where am I called upon already—or where might I step up and serve—as a peacemaker? What practical things are required of me to work toward peace in these situations? Would I benefit from a class in nonviolent communication? Do I need to inventory and seriously examine my own divisive vocabulary?

EPILOGUE

WHY THE RESISTANCE TO CONFIRMATION?

You Deserve to be Heard

Every one of us either *is* a teenager or young adult, or *knows* a teenager or young adult, or at least *has been* at some time a teenager or young adult. The emerging and early young adult years have long been a time of challenging transition, and even more so today. On all fronts, the difficult work of growing into one's fuller self can be exhausting, confusing, and intimidating. Wherever you find yourself on this spectrum—in the throes of emerging adulthood or well settled into a groove in later years—the following insights hopefully will offer understanding and encouragement as you undergo the lifelong spiritually maturing work of your anointing in Confirmation.

The Young Adult Challenge

To be emerging socially into young adulthood today means that a young person likely becomes a living, breathing complex of contradictions. Our contemporary culture has exploited this "complex" with multibillion dollar industries—from fashion to personal electronics, from cars to sports and video game entertainment—that prey on the human insecurities of identity and inclusion that seem to coalesce into what has come to be known as the "youth cult."

But this alien and alienating youth cult may be as much market hype as lived reality. Further, it denies a core truth of a young person's being, and that core truth is this: You cannot fall out of God's heart or God's providence, no matter what you experience or what you feel, and no matter what others might tell you. Nor can you escape God's endless yearning for you to be completely and wholeheartedly alive in Christ Jesus. God's love has a hold on each of us from well before our first breath to well beyond our last. Accepting this truth and allowing it to shape every dimension of your life is what it means to emerge spiritually from youth into adulthood.

The Holy Spirit does not abandon us and leave us on our own from, say, age twelve to about age thirty. God has nothing to gain by abandoning such youthful imagination, spunk, and spirit. The world needs what God has given to young people precisely at that stage in life. The sacrament of Confirmation blows open the doors from the inside out, setting young people—yes, even young people—free to be God's generous channels of grace and goodness in this world.

Still, many young people—and many not-so-young people—have days when they want to resist this whole business of being conformed to Christ, or may want to pick and choose the parts of their life in which they are willing to be conformed. Or they may mistakenly believe that their life is too ordinary for God to bother all that much. Why the resistance to the deeper grace of this anointing? Let's take a look at the two most cited reasons why youth, young adults, and even older adults resist giving themselves to the full power of their anointing in Confirmation.

Reasons for Push-back

The first and most frequent reason young people give for not wanting to be confirmed, or for resisting the self-giving way of life which honest relationship with the risen Lord requires, is this: *I don't believe in God.* The myth stubbornly persists that if you "don't believe in God" you are somehow released from the obligation to live a morally engaged and Christ-centered life. For some people, sadly, this myth can persist through the better part of life. The logic seems airtight: I don't believe in God, so therefore I am dismissed from the obligation to follow all those rules.

I could quickly reply: "But God believes in you"—which is truer than we may realize. God, in fact, not only believes in each of us, but is fully invested in each of us and is *counting* on each of us to give flesh-and-blood, here-and-now expression to God's redeeming love. Of course, God is GOD, and is capable of accomplishing all things by whatever means, whether you sign up or log in, or not. But I know for certain one thing that God is incapable of accomplishing. God is incapable of doing anything that lacks divine passion. Each of us exists and is sustained purely by the grace of this divine passion. Nothing, in fact, exists outside of it.

God indeed believes in us, and has believed in us enough to desire us into being. Furthermore, God has invested everything in us, through the life, death, and resurrection of Jesus, the well-beloved Son. The argument, "I don't believe in God," just does not carry weight. So those who do not believe in God may wish to honestly reconsider the real contents of their disbelief. The Holy Spirit is as close to us and as vital to us and as irrepressible as our own breath. The Holy Spirit is as steadfast within us as the beating of our own heart.

Still, a young person might look me in the eye and say again, with a little more force in the voice, as though I had not correctly heard, "I don't believe in God."

I would take this insistence as an invitation to talk, or perhaps as a plea to be listened to and finally heard. And I would ever so gently ask, *Can you tell me about the "God" you don't believe in?* Maybe no one has ever asked young people this question. Maybe young people have never expressed their unbelief in God in real words that others and even they themselves could hear. Now, in conversation, we may enter together into the work of dismantling a bogus god who would be quite content to have hearts and souls closed off to the one God who is unexplainable love and mercy, who is infinitely creative and personally invested in each person's everlasting joy. We humans are good at heaping blame onto God. Blaming God for the way things are is far easier to do than taking responsibility, as God's anointed ones, for our lives and for our world.

It very well may be that the "God" a young person professes to not believe in is a "God" I don't believe in, either. Young people who reject "God" may actually be on to something that is spiritually very important: dismantling a false god in order to enter into the real divine Mystery. That kind of spiritual wrestling is crucial to the inner workings of emerging faith. Genuine conversation and a real listening ear, and a "listening heart," may be the most spiritually meaningful gift that any of us can give to a young person—or a person of any age—who is wrestling with belief in God.

And if I ask you to tell me about the God you do *not* believe in, then I owe you some honest conversation about the God I *do* believe in. And we need to be in conversation until the words I speak find a way to resonate with meaning and encouragement and life within you. I owe a clean and clear expression of my Christian faith to those who are riddled with doubt. The words in the First Letter of St. Peter are clear and instructive: "Always be ready to give an explanation to anyone who asks you for a reason for your hope" (1 Peter 3:15).

The second most cited reason that youth, young adults, and even older adults offer for resisting the full anointing of Confirmation is this: *I'm not ready.*

But I wonder, can you tell me what "ready" looks like? Was that teenage girl of Nazareth—the young Virgin Mary—ready to become pregnant in the way the angel cryptically described to her, when she was betrothed but not yet fully given in marriage to her beloved Joseph? In a heartbeat she had to get ready not only for extraordinary motherhood but for the possibility of being stoned to death in the town square for bearing a child outside of wedlock, or at least not far enough into wedlock to satisfy the law. "I'm not ready" was not in her vocabulary.

For any of us, what will "ready" actually look like? God may have plans for your life that do not look like the plans you have pictured. Will your day of "ready" arrive with your name on it? Will it catch you by surprise? What if your notion of "ready" is different from God's notion of "ready"? If God deems that you are ready and you insist that you are not, who is out of step? Not God. As Jesus told his disciples, "Therefore, stay awake! For you do not know on which day your Lord will come" (Matthew 24:42). "Being ready" is not the same as understanding the details of how your future will play out. None of us is given the details, but every one of us is given the assignment to live a life fully anointed in the risen Christ. Each of us carries with us God's pledge to see us through, because God has anointed each one of us for a purpose that will be fulfilled, because it is *God's* purpose.

A Grown-up's Response

If you honestly confide in me all the reasons why you—no matter your age—feel that you are not ready for the full grace and anointing of Confirmation, then I owe you some honest talk about the ways I have felt unready for many of the challenges that have come my way since I was confirmed. If it were up to me, if I were here in this world acting on my own, I absolutely assure you that I would not feel ready to stand or to act in the place of the living Christ Jesus. But I am not in this world acting on my own. In Baptism and Confirmation I, like you, have received the Holy Spirit, a power far greater than myself. I have come to trust the words of St. Paul: "I live, no longer I, but Christ lives in me" (Galatians 2:20). These are not easy words. In fact, these words are spiritually sobering. I trust these words not because I understand them but because they resonate, they "ring true," at that place within me which belongs to God alone.[185] St. Paul further admonishes that my life is not my own, "[f]or you have been purchased at a price"—the price of the blood of the Lamb.[186]

With this sacrament of Confirmation, none of us is expected to really "get" it. How can we understand the mystery of our anointing? It is a mighty work of God which prepares us for a lifetime of giving ourselves consistently and wholeheartedly to the mystery of life in Christ, revealing the reign of God in our twenty-first century world. We do this work together, and in absolute trust that the Holy Spirit will lead us, that God will not abandon us.

You are anointed for a purpose. And this is what your life is for—for the unfolding of that purpose and your unique and lovely ways of revealing the reign of God.

Go *now,* and in peace!

---

[185] Thomas Merton writes about this place within, this point within the human soul which "belongs entirely to God" and which he describes as *le point vierge,* or the inviolable place within the soul which cannot be defiled or manipulated by human intention. See Merton, *Conjectures of a Guilty Bystander,* 146.

[186] See 1 Corinthians 6:19–20.

132

BIBLIOGRAPHY

Catechism of the Catholic Church, Second edition, English translation. Washington, DC: United States Catholic Conference, 1997.

Chittister, Joan, OSB. *Wisdom Distilled from the Daily: Living the Rule of St. Benedict Today.* San Francisco: HarperSanFrancisco, 1991.

Christian Prayer: The Liturgy of the Hours. Psalm texts except Psalm 95 from *The Psalms: A New Translation.* The Grail (England), 1963. New York: Catholic Book Publishing, 1976.

Clarke, John, OCD, trans. *Letters of St. Thérèse of Lisieux, Volume II: 1890– 1897.* Washington, DC: ICS Publications, 1988.

Cunningham, Lawrence, ed., with introduction. *Thomas Merton: Spiritual Master.* New York: Paulist, 1992.

Day, Dorothy. *The Long Loneliness: The Autobiography of Dorothy Day.* San Francisco: Harper & Row, 1952, 1981.

Dear, John, SJ. *Living Peace: A Spirituality of Contemplation and Action.* New York: Image Doubleday, 2001.

Farrington, Debra. *One Like Jesus: Conversations on the Single Life.* Chicago: Loyola Press, 1999.

Flannery, Austin, OP, gen. ed. *Vatican Council II, Volume 1: The Conciliar and Post Conciliar Documents. Pastoral Constitution on the Church in the Modern World,* 903–1001. Northport, NY: Costello Publishing, 1975, 1998.

Holy Bible: New International Version. Grand Rapids, MI: Zondervan Bible Publishers, 1973, 1996.

Hughes, Kathleen, RSCJ. *The Monk's Tale: A Biography of Godfrey Diekmann, OSB.* Collegeville, MN: The Liturgical Press, 1991.

Killen, Patricia O'Connell, and John de Beer. *The Art of Theological Reflection.* New York: Crossroad, 2002.

Kreider, Alan F. "Learning to Live Like Christians." *The Sign of Peace,* Spring 2010, 21–24.

Merton, Thomas. *Conjectures of a Guilty Bystander.* In *Thomas Merton, Spiritual Master,* edited with introduction by Lawrence S. Cunningham, 121–164. New York: Paulist, 1992.

Metz, Johannes. *Poverty of Spirit.* Mahwah, NJ: Paulist Press, 1968, 1998.

Moore, Mary Sharon. *Christian Celibate Life: Discerning the Authentic Gift,* MP-3 audio compact disc. Eugene, OR: Awakening Vocations, 2010.

_____. *Moving in God's Direction: Essentials of Christ-centered Spiritual and Vocational Direction.* Eugene, OR: Awakening Vocations, 2012.

_____. "Obliged by Love: Rediscovering the Real Obligation of Sunday Mass." *Today's Catholic Teacher,* April-May 2011, 84–85.

_____. *Touching the Reign of God: Bringing Theological Reflection to Daily Life.* Eugene, OR: Wipf and Stock, 2009.

Neafsey, John. *A Sacred Voice is Calling: Personal Vocation and Social Conscience.* Maryknoll NY: Orbis, 2006.

Nemeck, Francis Kelly, OMI, and Marie Theresa Coombs. *Called by God: A Theology of Vocation and Lifelong Commitment.* Eugene, OR: Wipf and Stock, 2001.

_____. *Discerning Vocations to Marriage, Celibacy and Singlehood.* Eugene, OR: Wipf and Stock, 2001.

New American Bible. Grand Rapids, MI: Catholic World Press, 1987.

Newman, Blessed John Henry Cardinal. Meditation 299 (1), "Hope in God-Creator," March 6, 1848. http://www.newmanreader.org/works. meditations/meditations9.html#doctrine1 (accessed July 15, 2011).

Prejean, Helen, CSJ. "The Promise of Restorative Justice." Sponsored by the Appropriate Dispute Resolution Center, the Clark Honors College, and the Savage Endowment for International Relations and Peace, University of Oregon School of Law, Eugene, OR, October 19, 2010.

Rolheiser, Ronald. *The Holy Longing: The Search for a Christian Spirituality.* New York: Doubleday, 1999.

Roman Missal: Second Edition. New York: Catholic Book Publishing, 1985.

Roman Missal: Third Edition. Washington, DC: ICEL, 2010.

Salinger, J. D. *Franny and Zooey.* New York: Bantam, 1961, 1969.

Simon, Paul. "The Only Living Boy in New York." In Simon and Garfunkel, *Bridge Over Troubled Water.* New York: Columbia/Legacy, 88697 82724 1, 2010 (1969).

Straub, Gerard Thomas. *The Narrow Path: Walking Toward Peace and Nonviolence with John Dear, SJ,* video. Burbank, CA: The San Damiano Foundation, 2007.

Strong, James, STD, LLD. *The New Strong's Exhaustive Concordance of the Bible.* Nashville: Thomas Nelson Publishers, 1996.

Teilhard de Chardin, Pierre, SJ. *Hymn of the Universe.* New York: Harper & Row, 1961.

West, Christopher. *Theology of the Body for Beginners: A Basic Introduction to Pope John Paul II's Sexual Revolution.* West Chester, PA: Ascension Press, 2004.

Whyte, David. *Crossing the Unknown Sea: Work as a Pilgrimage of Identity.* New York: Riverhead Books, 2001.

_____. *The Three Marriages: Reimagining Work, Self and Relationship.* New York: Riverhead Books, 2009.

SCRIPTURE CITATIONS
AND REFERENCES

Old Testament

Genesis
- **1**:26–30; **3**:9; **33**:23–33

Deuteronomy
- **6**:5; **24**:1–4

Joshua
- **24**:15

1 Samuel
- **16**:12–13

2 Samuel
- **5**:3

1 Kings
- **3**:9

Psalms
- **23**; **90**:17; **92**; **108**:13

Isaiah
- **50**:4–5; **61**:1–2

Joel
- **1**:13–14; **2**:17

New Testament

Matthew
- **3**:13–17; **5**:3–16, 31–32, 43–48; **6**:9–15, 30–33; **7**:29; **8**:26; **9**:1–8; **10**:1, 37; **11**:29–30; **13**:24, 33, 44–47; **14**:22–33; **18**:21–35; **19**:3–9, 11–12; **21**:12–13, 23–27; **22**:37–39; **24**:42, 45; **25**:31–46; **26**:39, 51–52

Mark
- **1**:9–11, 22; **2**:1–12; **3**:13–15; **4**:21–22; **5**:1–20; **6**:7; **8**:29; **9**:50; **10**:17–22; **11**:15–18, 27–33; **12**:29–31; **14**:36, 55–64

Luke
- **2**:49; **3**:21–22; **4**:16–21, 32; **5**:17–26; **6**:20–49; **7**:36–50; **8**:16–17; **9**:1–2, 62; **10**:1–12, 21, 25–37; **11**:2–4, 33; **13**:21; **14**:34–35; **15**:11–32; **17**:21; **19**:45–46; **20**:1–8; **22**:42, 50–51; **23**:34, 43, 46

John
- **1**:5, 32–33; **2**:14–16; **4**:13–14, 25, 34; **5**:43; **6**:35, 60–68; **8**:3–12, 26; **9**:5; **10**:10–12, 15, 30; **11**:41–42; **12**:8, 24, 44–46; **13**:3–7, 15; **14**:2–3, 9–10, 12, 26–27; **15**:4a, 9, 16; **17**:6–15, 20–24; **18**:10–11, 37; **20**:15, 17, 19–23, 26; **21**:18

Acts of the Apostles
- **2**:1–4; **4**:27; **5**:28–40; **8**:26–40; **10**:38

Romans
- **5**:7–8; **8**:26–27, 29; **12**:2; **14**:8

1 Corinthians

- **1**:23; **2**:9, 16; **6**:19–20; **12**:12, 27; **15**:28

2 Corinthians
- **3**:18; **4**:4; **5**:15

Galatians
- **2**:20

Ephesians
- **2**:14–15; **4**:1, 4–5, 13

Philippians
- **2**:5–7; **3**:10–11; **4**:6–7

Colossians
- **1**:15, 17, 19–20a; **3**:23

1 Thessalonians
- **5**:17

1 Peter
- **1**:3; **3**:15; **5**:8–9

2 Peter
- **1**:10

INDEX

anointed: for a purpose, 2, 5, 43, 58, 98, 109, 122–23, 132; Jesus as Anointed One, 44; living the anointed life, 2, 10, 77, 122; to "be someone," 80; to "do something," 80; washed and, 15

anointing: definition of, 43–44; in Confirmation, 46; mission and, 47n74; sacramental, 2, 11n6, 127; vocational dimension of, 96, 102, 106, 109, 124

apostleship, 63; Jesus as preeminent Apostle, 12; nature of, 73

authentic self-in-God, 2, 13, 27n36, 40–41, 94, 96; Confirmation and, 18; humility and, 40; spiritual freedom and, 43, 47; vocational lifestyle and, 94, 96

authority: definition of, 37; divine, 4; flowing from God, 37; Holy Spirit and, 38; humility and, 39, 41; not license, 37; of anointing, 64; Jesus' own, 38, 115n162, 117; of peacemaking, 113; to forgive sins, 118; to intercede, 53; standing in Jesus' place with, 35, 39, 58, 124

awakening: as existential waking up, 56n91; as interior waking up, 20n23; as waking up of church, 34; from sleep of inhumanity, 56n91; interior, 56n91; of parish community, 71n104; of social conscience, 92, 123

Baptism: anointing in, 3; as "one-time event," 10; Christian community and, 4; garments of, 10; God's calling and, 11, 29; Holy Spirit and, 36, 73, 132; Jesus' baptism, 44; relationship with God and, 13; sacrament of, 2; standing in the place of Jesus and, 35. *See also* sacraments of initiation

baptismal role of king, 52, 152; as divine governance, 55; as wise steward, 56; vocational connection, 56

baptismal role of priest, 52; as intercession, 53; vocational connection, 56

baptismal role of prophet, 52, 54; seeing through prophetic lens, 54; vocational connection, 56

calling: celibate life and, 87n121, 89n126; Confirmation and, 31; discerning vocation and, 1–5, 106n147; discerning vocational lifestyles, 81, 92; distinct from career, 97–100, 103; faithful response to, 15; five steps in discerning, 104–109; fruitfulness in, 57, 100n134, 104n140; gifting and, 16; in context of Christian community, 16; in new stages of life, 67; nature of God's, 79–80, 102; prayer and, 105n143; relationship with God and, 22, 26–

27, 47; to celibate life, 87–90; to
Christian married life, 84–87; to
singlehood, 81–84
career: definition of, 98–99; demands
of, 100n134; distinct from calling,
97–98, 103; Jesus on, 100–101
Catechism of the Catholic Church,
10n3; abbreviated as *CCC,* 46n73,
69n101, 84n114
Catherine of Siena, Saint, 109
celibacy: as charism, 86n120, 89; as
Christian vocational lifestyle, 87–
90; as requirement, 88, 89n125;
confused with singlehood, 81–82;
definition of, 87; lay celibates, 88;
no automatic connection to
priesthood or religious life, 89;
spiritual fruitfulness and, 89. *See
also* vocational lifestyle
chastity: definition of, 83; in
singlehood, 83;
Chittister, Joan, 27n35
chrism, 7, 44, 46
Christian community: as community
of faith, 49, 69; as dynamic
relationship, 14, 70–72; challenge
and encouragement of, 69–70, 72;
collective anointing of, 4, 64;
personal acknowledgment and,
70–71; place within, 3, 7, 22, 49,
64, 73; resources and, 70, 72; role
of, 15, 16, 43; St. Paul and early,
123
Christian Prayer (The Liturgy of the
Hours), 44n66, 99n133, 113n158.
See also Liturgy of the Hours
christification: as life in Christ, 19;
definition of, 18–20; in the
writings of Merton, 19–20; in the
writings of Teilhard, 19. *See also*
Merton; Teilhard
Clarke, John, 25n33
Confirmation: anointed for a purpose
in, 5; anointed to be someone in,
96, 103; anointed to do something
in, 96; as "one-time event," 10, 18,
73; as sacrament of initiation, 11;
as Yes, 4, 14, 16, 20, 42, 73, 99,
103; Baptism and, 2, 35, 53, 55;
conformation and, 60–61; divine
indwelling and, 26; Eucharist and,
4; resistance to, 66, 127–131;

sacrament of, 9–16, 22, 46; sealed
in the Holy Spirit in, 36, 48;
spiritual adulthood and, 62–63, 73;
trajectory of anointed life and, 12.
See also sacraments of initiation
conformation, being conformed to
Christ, 60–61
conscience, personal: formation of,
91, 123; listening with the ear of,
54; spiritual maturity and, 92
conscience, social: formation of, 91;
listening with the ear of, 54;
spiritual maturity and, 92, 123
consecration: through sacramental
anointing, 2, 35, 45
Coombs, Marie Theresa, 12n7,
80n109, 85n117, 89n126. *See also*
Nemeck, Francis Kelly
Cunningham, Lawrence, 20n22

Day, Dorothy, 88n124, 119n174
de Beer, John, 72n107, 108n148. *See
also* Killen, Patricia O'Connell
Dear, John, 101n137, 115
discernment, vocational: assumptions
in, 89n126; definition of, 90; five
steps to, 104–109; not same as
"deciding," 90–91; patterns of
effectiveness in, 97; process of,
89n126, 93; vocational lifestyle
and, 21n24, 79–80, 87
discipleship, 113
dying and rising, 29, 105n143. *See
also* paschal mystery

Eucharist: as spiritual nourishment,
64, 70; Baptism, Confirmation
and, 4, 11; remembering in, 46;
repeatable sacrament, 10;
sacrament of, 3, 15. *See also*
sacraments of initiation

faithfulness and obedience, 109; as
requirement for relationship with
God, 50; as spiritual qualities, 30;
missional separation and, 68
Farrington, Debra, 82n111
for God, 12–14, 93. *See also* from
God; returning to God
forgiveness: as unexplainable release
from bondage, 116; in relation to
healing, 114n159, 116nn166–168;

Jesus and, 53, 112, 114; peacemaking and, 114, 116 from God, 12–14, 23, 49. *See also* for God; returning to God

God's desiring: in current circumstances, 102; of each person, 13; through vocational lifestyle, 80; trusting in, 104; within the self, 24. *See also* God's willing
God's willing, 13, 15, 58, 100; discerned through "a listening heart," 22n29; discerning, 35, 77, 93, 104; missional separation and, 68; obstacles to embracing, 82n112; perfection of, 84; signs of, 90, 92; vocation and, 56.;

Holy Orders: sacrament of, 10; as "one-time event," 10
Hughes, Kathleen, 33n41
humility: Beatitudes and, 39; conforming to Christ's humility, 39n55; definition of, 39; in relationship with God, 50, 54; sacramental anointing and, 35, 37, 55; of God, 40; of Jesus, 40–41;

imagination, anointed, 54, 72; in Christian life, 105n143; mission field and, 64; of Jesus, 41; work and, 98; spiritual life, 48, 53, 56–57
Incarnation: as aspect of God's calling, 31; centrality of in Christian life, 105; implications of, 34
intentionality: in openness to God's plan, 104; in prayer, 50; in sacramental life, 47

Jesus, standing in the place of, 12n8, 16, 35n45, 58, 103, 124

Killen, Patricia O'Connell, 72n107, 108n148. *See also* de Beer, John
Kreider, Alan F., 119n174, 120n176

Liturgy of the Hours, 23n31, 25n32, 105n143. *See also Christian Prayer*

love: as justice, 115; as right relationship, 115; as sacramental anointing, 2, 45, 109; at the service of peace, 116; expressed by Jesus, 21, 36, 42, 67, 112, 114, 117; God's, 4, 14, 22, 40–41, 51, 55, 84, 105, 113, 124, 128; in marriage covenant, 85; in mature Christian life, 11, 30; of enemies, 116

marriage, Christian, assumptions in discerning, 89n126; definition of, 84; discerning the vocational lifestyle of, 79–82; divorce and, 85n116, 86n118; expression of God's covenant love, 84; in relation to celibate life, 86; in relation to single life, 83–84; theology of the body and, 84. *See also* vocational lifestyle
Matrimony, sacrament of: as "one-time event," 10; defined in *Catechism of the Catholic Church,* 84n114
Merton, Thomas: in *Conjectures of a Guilty Bystander,* 20n22, 101n136, 132n185; Catholic Peace Fellowship and, 119n174. *See also* christification
Metz, Johannes, 23n30
midlife crisis, 65, 98n132
missional separation: as vocational separation, 66–69; definition of, 67; in Jesus' life, 68
Moore, Mary Sharon, 4n2, 25n32, 30n39, 69n101, 72n107

Neafsey, John, 56n91, 91n129
Nemeck, Francis Kelly, 12n7, 80n109, 85n117, 89n126. *See also* Coombs, Marie Theresa
Newman, John Henry Cardinal, Blessed, 43n63

paschal mystery, 29, 105n143. *See also* dying and rising
peacemaking: as expression of reign of God, 34; as responsibility, 114; as sign of conversion, 115, 119; as vocational imperative, 88, 109, 114, 124; Beatitudes and, 112–13,

118; conscience, and 123; forgiveness and, 114–15; in the early church, 119, 121; intentional, 121; Jesus as model of, 36; none apart from risen Christ, 123n182; nonviolence and, 115, 119; powerlessness and, 113; preeminence of, 120; reconciliation and, 116, 120; restorative justice and, 115
Pentecost, 34, 46
personhood, authentic, 60, 80–81;
prayer: as "inexpressible groanings," 23, 25; authentic, 23; intercessory, 24, 88;
Prejean, Helen, 20n23

rebellion, personal: in contrast to missional separation, 68; of King Solomon, 65
returning to God, 12, 14–15. *See also* for God; from God
Rolheiser, Ronald, 106n146
Roman Missal: Second Edition, 37n48, 120; Third Edition, 37n48, 120n179

sacraments of initiation, 2, 4, 10–11, 16. *See also* Baptism; Confirmation; Eucharist
Salinger, J. D., 21n26
Second Vatican Council, 33
singlehood: as "incompleteness," 82; as vocational lifestyle, 81–84; Catholic matchmaking Web sites

and, 82; confused with celibacy, 80n108, 81–82; definition of, 81; openness to the possibility of marriage, 81, 83. *See also* vocational lifestyle
spiritual adulthood, 62, 64, 71
Straub, Gerard Thomas, 101n137
Strong, James, 21n25, 44n65, 111, 112nn152, 154, 155

Teilhard de Chardin, Pierre, 19, 33. *See also* christification
theological reflection, 72, 108
Thérèse of the Child Jesus, Saint, 25
trajectory: career, 99n133; of life, 2, 62, 103; of the church, 33–34
transformation: sacramental anointing and, 39; spiritual work of, 61, 83n113
trust: absolute, 41–42, 117–18, 132; radical, 41, 117

vocational lifestyle, 79; definition of, 81; discernment of, 80; five encouragements for discerning, 92–94. *See also* celibacy; marriage, Christian; singlehood

West, Christopher, 84n115
wholeheartedness, 28n37; as sign of vocation, 102, 128, 132; as way of Christian living, 97, 100, 104, 107, 109, 116
Whyte, David, 28n37; 93n131, 100n134, 102n138

Mary Sharon Moore is founding director of Awakening Vocations and an active writer and speaker on the nature of God's calling. Her spiritual and vocational direction practice spans the United States, Canada, and beyond.

Anointed for a Purpose is the ideal gift and a great resource for those coming into the church, for those returning to the church, and for young adults preparing for Confirmation or becoming established in their young adult faith.

Bulk discounts start at 10 copies. More at www.awakeningvocations.com/store

Personal and parish resources for spiritual and vocational development can be found at www.awakeningvocations.com as well. Visit us on the Web, or call us toll-free during usual business hours: 1.888.687.2046 (Pacific).

Also from Awakening Vocations:

- *Moving in God's Direction: Essentials of Christ-centered Spiritual and Vocational Direction.* An in-depth look at this powerful means of spiritual and vocational growth, *Moving in God's Direction* is designed for spiritual directors, directees, and those who simply want to know more about all of the dimensions of life that matter in the work of spiritual growth.

- *Touching the Reign of God: Bringing Theological Reflection to Daily Life.* This collection of thirteen gemlike essays brings circumstances of life into laser-sharp focus, and reveals the power of Christian imagination and understanding in detecting God's movement in both action and prayer.

- *Anointed for a Purpose:* 10 sessions, 5 hours, 1 MP3 CD, with Mary Sharon Moore, and host Terry Amato. Recorded at KBVM.FM, Catholic Broadcasting Northwest.

- *Christian Celibate Life: Discerning the Authentic Gift:* 13 sessions, 6-1/2 hours, 1 MP3 CD, with Mary Sharon Moore, and host Terry Amato. Recorded at KBVM.FM, Catholic Broadcasting Northwest.

Awakening Vocations | 4150 Oak Street | Eugene OR 97405
541.687.2046 | 1.888.687.2046 | www.awakeningvocations.com